LIVES IN THE MAKING

The Story of a Manufacturing Family

KUNIYASU SAKAI
As Told to David Russell

Intercultural Group
New York & Tokyo

Edited by Kenichi Miyashita
Jacket Design by Ryuichi Minakawa
Published by Integrace Japan Co., Ltd.
Daiichi Ginroku Bldg., 3F, 6-11-10, Ginza, Chuo-ku, Tokyo, 104, Japan

Sakai, Kuniyasu, 1928-
[Karakurishi no matsuei. English]
Lives in the making : the story of a manufacturing family
/ Kuniyasu Sakai. As told to David Russell.
p. cm. — (ICG pocketbusiness book)
ISBN 1-881267-04-0
1. Industrialists—Japan—Biography. 2. Sakai Family.
3. Japan—Manufacturers—History. 4. Tokyo (Japan)—Industries—
History.
I. Title. II. Series.
HC461.5.A2S27513 1992
338.092'252—dc20
[B]   92-22761 CIP

Printed and Bound in Japan

2CM

Praise For "Lives In The Making"

"This is essential reading for anyone who believes the Japanese are 'faceless.' Here instead is a group of thoroughly believable individuals, all engaged in the running of small businesses... A fascinating insight into their hearts and minds, as well as into Japanese business practices."

Naohiro Amaya
Former Councillor of MITI
(Ministry of International Trade and Industry)

CONTENTS

Foreword   5

Part I: The Sakai Family   11
Introduction: The World of Metal and
                    Wood   12
Artisans of Edo   16
Tarokichi   22
The Golden Leaf   30
A Woman's Sacrifice   41
Naokichi   47
The Growth of Industry   57
An Interesting Neighbor   66
A New Life   71
On His Own   77
Part II: Kuniyasu Remembers   89
Putting Our Lives Back Together   90
A 'Sun' Is Born   97
Hiroshi   103
Kids, Cars, Bankers and Work   107
First Signs of Success   115
Death (and Birth) of a Salesman   121
The Taiyo Game System   128
Employees   134
Diversification   139
It Helps to Know the Future   146
Naokichi's Legacy   150

Afterword   155

Foreword

One of the most important characteristics that distinguishes man from the other animals is the ability to use tools. Certain animals may wish to dispute this, but let them take it up with the anthropologists — I am content to know that the relationship between man and tools is older than that between man and language. Even if our early ancestors did nothing more sophisticated than use a stick to knock fruit from a tree, the stick was a proper "tool" and employing it was "work." Since that time, tools have changed considerably, but man's need for them has not.

I will admit at the outset to having an unabashed fondness for tools, and for their offspring, machines. Even as a child I loved to make things, to take things apart and try to put them back together (not always successfully). Fortunately, I grew up in a household where tinkering with machinery was considered good, healthy behavior for a child. My father ran a precision tool shop, his own father was a noted inventor, and our family had been making tools and implements for generations before that. Thus, I inherited a love of making things just as surely as I inherited my physical features.

When I was 19 and had a chance to start my own company, I did not go into making things (for reasons I shall explain later), but into industrial painting. I was not trying to escape my family's calling, merely to survive in difficult times. Yet one thing led to another, and before long I found my business drifting back towards the mechanical, as if pulled by some unseen force. My little company grew and spun off dozens of new companies, but our main business remained in manufacturing. Today I oversee a dynamic group of firms which makes everything from the simplest electronic parts to state-of-the-art equipment. You have never seen a "Sakai" brand computer or laser printer or color copier because I do not put my name on my work. I make thousands of different products for Japan's biggest electronics firms (think of any company that comes to mind —I make something for all of them), and you buy my products with their brand name.

The simple fact is, I make things because I like to make them, because I feel that quality manufacturing is an art, and thus a credit to the manufacturer. I don't care whether he's a man in a worn shop apron turning a lathe in a machine shop or a white-suited technician operating computer-driven inspection equipment in an IC "clean room"—to me they're all making things, and they should take pride in their work. My employees agree: they don't need to see their company name on the finished products, only to know that they make the best there is. I am very grateful that the Almighty let me stray from the world of manufacturing only to bring me back where I belong. And I know that my father and his father and his father, too, would be proud to see another generation of the Sakai family devoting his life to making things. It is more than a family tradition: it is our destiny.

Whenever people used to ask about my work or about how our Bunsha Group of companies came to be, I would begin by saying "After the war I started a painting company...," but I soon learned that this explanation was not very helpful to my listeners. Especially my foreign friends, who, knowing little of what Japan was like half a century ago, always found it difficult to understand what led me to do the things I have done. Gradually I discovered that the best way for me to explain both my own and my firm's beginnings is to go back into the past and set the stage for what was to follow. As you may imagine, this is by far the most satisfying way to present things from my point of view, although I realize that it is also quite time-consuming, and surely has caused many a listener to wonder if there shouldn't be a law forbidding old men from rambling on about the past ad infinitum.

Thus, to spare my future listeners the lengthy tale, yet to be able once and for all to tell the full story of my family and how we came to be, I have decided to record our history in a book for all to see. It begins with a bit of an introduction to the world of crafts, partly because I am still fascinated by the work of ancient carpenters and partly because my ancestors worked in a related field as blacksmiths. As Japan began to change, our family became hardware dealers, then machinists, then inventors, and eventually a child was born who could do none of these worthy things. This child, talentless though he may have been, was blessed with an understanding family and a stalwart best friend, and with their unwavering support he built not a machine, but a company. And from one company he built dozens, and from this experience developed a philosophy of company management that will continue long after he is gone.

I suppose the truth is that I enjoy history, and so a journey into the past is always a pleasure. I love to talk about my company and how it was started, but to do so inevitably involves an explanation of my father's business. And to talk about his business leads to a discussion of his father, a machinist of remarkable talent. And to put my grandfather's work in perspective requires an understanding of what Japan was like before and during its belated industrial revolution. In other words, I must ask the reader's indulgence, to wander with me just a bit in earlier times. I know that many of you have little knowledge of, and perhaps little interest in old Japan, while many others only wish to hear about my corporate group as it exists today. To such readers I can only say that this is not the book for you. The second volume in this series tells how my original company (Taiyo Industry) grew into what is now the Bunsha Group. It also explains the management philosophy that I developed along the way. For those interested in this story, I recommend the next volume, entitled Bunsha.

Kuniyasu Sakai
Tokyo, 1991

Part I
THE SAKAI FAMILY

Introduction:
The World of Metal and Wood

Despite the differences in Japanese and European history, I suspect the evolution of tools, and thus of crafts, followed more or less similar patterns, for artisans and craftsmen tend to evolve in the same way regardless of place or time.

Needless to say, people in both societies originally made all their tools and performed all their work by themselves (which is hard to imagine these days). Gradually, it became apparent that some people were more adept at making certain kinds of tools or at performing certain kinds of work. In the course of things, various people came to specialize in particular skills. So, for example, the carpenter, the blacksmith, the cooper and the candlemaker came into being. It was quite natural for particular kinds of work to become the province of specialists. It was equally natural for the manufacture of tools for each kind of work to be left to these or to other specialists.

As people moved into the nascent cities, workers in the same trade were drawn together by the common needs to obtain raw materials and to sell their products. From this centralization of specialized labor and the introduction of more sophisticated tools (called machines), modern industry emerged.

Two trades that were born in antiquity but survived and flourished over the centuries were those of the carpenter and blacksmith. From ancient times, smiths and carpenters were bound together by the nature of their work. In many cases, the tools each used were a combination of their common primary materials, wood and metal. The larger parts were of course made of wood. Blades and other parts requiring sharpness or hardness were either made of or reinforced with iron. It was natural for artisans in these two fields to work closely together.

I have a special interest in smiths because my ancestors centuries ago were engaged in that profession. The main work of a smith was to heat iron in a furnace, temper it, and forge it into a desired quality and shape. This produced excellent hard or sharp objects. The smith might also melt metal and cast it in a mold, perhaps to make larger items or those with intricate designs (what we call foundry). In ancient Japan, there were as many kinds of smiths (*kaji*) as there were metal objects to create. Some specialized in making farming tools, while some made the metal utensils of daily life. Others made helmets, swords, or gun barrels (despite all the pictures you have seen of sword-toting samurai, Japan had a very active industry producing both musket and cannon in the 16th century). Yet neither the gunsmiths nor the swordsmiths were destined to survive. The former profession fell from favor early on, while the latter was abolished a little over a century ago as Japan began to modernize. Almost all of these exceptional craftsmen turned their skills to the making of simple, metal utensils for home or farm use.

Like the smiths, the carpenters of old were divided into specialized areas such as house building, furniture making, watermill construction and shipbuilding. I find the work of these early carpenters as intriguing as others might find a detective novel. I have spent considerable time in museums, examining, for instance, the wooden gears of earlier centuries. I am fascinated to discover not only that very hard woods were used, but also that the wood was carved in such a way that the grain actually helped to reinforce the wheels and prevent wear. Moreover, the wheels were fit together so that pressure would be evenly applied to each wheel. I am amazed when I think of what marvellous men nurtured and passed on these crafts throughout the years.

In 1819, a watermill carpenter named Chojiro Nagai of the Village of Akagi in Gumma Prefecture built a theater stage using techniques he had learned while working on water-driven mills. The stage was roughly 30 feet wide by 22 feet deep and featured a mini-elevator for raising actors up onto the stage via a trapdoor. All of this was accomplished through the basic mechanics of simple, toothed gears. Gears of different sizes made it possible to change speeds instead of merely transferring motion. And by different placement of the gears, vertical, horizontal and angular motions were also possible. This was very important due to a difference in the way waterwheels were employed in Japan.

Of course, there were waterwheels in Europe even earlier than those in Japan, but differences in the two cultures meant differences in the way their machines were used. In the West, flour is ground in order to make bread, thus requiring a horizontal rotation for grinding. I suspect the miller in Franz Schubert's song "Die Schone Mullerin" ground rather than pounded his grain. In Japan, however, the preparation of rice requires a vertical pounding motion for husking and cleaning. Thus, Japanese carpenters had to be creative in adapting the horizontal power of the waterwheel.

In 1867, the Satsuma clan (of the southern island, Kyushu), were eager to improve their knowledge of mechanics, and so decided to import industrial techniques from abroad. They purchased a Western-style waterwheel and invited a British engineer to serve as their instructor. According to the records of the day, the wheel was a particularly efficient "Dutch-style wheel." With it, they opened a modern spinning and weaving factory. Somewhat late in terms of world history, Japan was beginning to develop what we would now call modern industry. But it was the work of the carpenters and smiths of old, the first mechanical engineers in Japan, that set the stage for this later industrial revolution.

Water power soon gave way to steam, and steam to gas and then to electricity. But the basic principles of the transmission of energy remained intact. The gears that were driven by a waterwheel two hundred years ago are essentially the same mechanism that propels your Honda down the highway. The tremendous power of the gasoline engine is significant only in that it can be harnessed to transfer rotation to an axle, that is, to turn gears just like a water wheel. The speed and power of the system have changed dramatically, but the principle that makes the machine work would be immediately comprehensible to a smith or a waterwheel carpenter of the early nineteenth century.

Artisans of Edo

I have long been a student of history—not only the history of invention, mind you, but also the history of my own city, Tokyo, which was known for centuries as Edo. As you have probably read, Edo was one of the largest, and in some ways most advanced cities of the pre-modern world. Even in the eighteenth century it had a population of over a million (making it larger than London or Paris at the time), an extensive network of highways, water works, and a postal system.

Edo rose from a small community to a town of prominence in 1582 when Ieyasu Tokugawa, the man who would become the first great Shogun, settled there. The Edo settlement began with civil engineering work, levelling the hills and filling in the lowlands. Over the next forty years the basic foundation of the city was laid out and the majestic Edo Castle completed. While much of the area near the castle was allotted to the various feudal lords who were loyal supporters of the Tokugawa family, the hills and marshes just east of the castle were given mainly to artisans. The area was called *shitamachi* or "downtown," a name which survives even today, although you won't find it on many maps.

If you look at an old map of Edo, you will notice that many of the smaller neighborhoods (*cho*) in shitamachi bear names like Nabe-cho (potter's town), Kaji-cho (smiths' town), Tate-daiku-cho (carpenters' town), and so on. Other place names indicate the dwellings of woodcutters, leatherworkers, bow-makers, tatami-makers, dyers, lacquerers, and even doll-makers. Many of these names still exist today although their practitioners are long since gone. If you walk through the old part of Tokyo, from Nihonbashi up through Kanda, you may wonder why a modern business district like Ningyo-cho (Dolls' town) has such a funny name, but to people in the area it is a reminder that the neighborhood's heritage extends back over 300 years.

These interesting place names indicate that to one side of Edo Castle, and not far from the residences of high-class samurai, there was a fairly large area devoted to the craftsmen who supplied both town and castle. These craftsmen passed their skills along from generation to generation, and many families continued to work in the same small shop in Kanda or its environs for centuries. Techniques were refined, but technologies remained basically the same—until the more enterprising among the workers began to hear of "new" technologies developing far away from their castle town.

Although the shoguns shut Japan off from the outside world, forbidding contact with the West after about 1640, foreign scholarship continued to seep into the country, mostly via Dutch traders who were granted special trading rights in Nagasaki on the island of Kyushu. Through the tiny window of this single, open port in the southernmost part of Japan, Western science began to filter into the country. As poor translations of Western books began to circulate, they fueled a desire to learn more about the new technologies emerging outside Japan.

The opportunity to see Western technologies up close came a century later, when the famous "black ships" of Commodore Perry arrived in the mid-nineteenth century, demanding that Japan open itself to international trade. The feudal lords of two southern fiefs then set out to construct steamboats on the model of western ships. This may well have been the beginning of heavy industry in Japan.

In a surprisingly short time new industries

developed and old ones, like the smiths, were transformed into something very different. Tiny, wooden shops on the back streets of Kanda were inadequate for these new businesses. The evolution of family-run shops into small factories meant a need for more space, not only for more workers, but also because the new businesses produced loud noises, bad smells and sometimes lots of steam, unlike their more "neighborly" predecessors. As a result, they had to leave Kanda. These craftsmen-turned-factory-owners wanted some open space not too far from the center of the city and close to water so they could transport their raw materials. One of the most important areas the settled in was a stretch of filled-in land south of the castle facing Tokyo Bay, known as Shibaura. Many of the workers from Kanda moved to Shibaura and the area soon came to be known as a home for newly developing industries. You already know the name of one of the most famous, a small company that started out in the 19th century as the Tanaka Workshop. Moving to the new area, the firm changed its name to the Shibaura Factory, and then, as it began producing more electronic products, to Tokyo Shibaura Electric. But nobody called it Tokyo Shibaura Electric; they shortened it by combining the first two words, and for decades the firm was known by its nickname. Only in recent times did the company officially change its name to match the old nickname: Toshiba.

This development in Shibaura was just one

of many, as workers from the Kanda district spread out in search of more space to develop their skills. Many in the mechanical trades moved to the south side of the city, while many of those working in the glass, leather, and chemical businesses moved north. In this way, Tokyo grew as an industrial community, and these specialized areas made it easier for workers in certain fields to gather, to procure materials as a group, and to market them more easily. In fact, the very existence of these areas attracted a steady flow of labor. Since the skills employed there could only be acquired by apprenticeship, young men anxious to learn a trade were drawn to the developing industrial towns.

My family were metalworkers in Edo. From long ago my ancestors had been smiths, makers of metal tools and weapons. One of our forebears several generations back made many of the implements used in one of the most famous of all episodes in both history and literature, a tale known in Japanese as *Chushingura*, and in English as "The Revenge of the 47 Loyal Samurai." The 47 samurai of the tale were forced to kill themselves after carrying out their mission, and were buried at a temple in Tokyo called Sengakuji, which is now our family temple. There is a small museum there which I visit occasionally. I can't help but marvel at the display of ancient iron implements. Which among them, I wonder, were the handiwork of my ancestor, Den'emon? On some quiet evenings, as I stand alone gazing at those handmade tools from 300 years ago, I feel transported, as if I were actually standing in a dark corner of his shop, watching him at work. I can almost feel the flames from his furnace and hear the sound of his bellows and the pounding of his hammer on the anvil.

Like many Japanese, our family history has been handed down orally, from generation to generation, and so the tale of the smith Den'emon's contribution to the revenge of the 47 samurai was told by his descendants every New Year for over ten generations at the family ceremony called "the Starting of the Bellows." For centuries, the head of our family has been called "Den'emon." The name was inherited by the first son, just as he became heir to the secret arts of the family. Upon attaining manhood, he had to undergo special training to learn the skills which were handed down only from father to son. When he took over the responsibilities of running the household, he also acquired the name of Den'emon.

Private vendettas aside, the Tokugawa era (the two and a half centuries of rule by the Shoguns) was a relatively peaceful time, and so there was less and less need for swords or other weapons except as decorations. My family, like many other smiths, devoted themselves exclusively to making agricultural tools, sickles, axes, plows, and household utensils.

Although my family were mere artisans, not aristocrats nor of the privileged samurai class, we know that my great-grandfather Den'emon had achieved some stature, as he married a woman from a very well-to-do home (it is said that she never learned the different types of Japanese coins until her marriage since she never needed money before then. And yet, being members of the artisan class, they were not permitted to use a family surname until 1870. At that time, a few years after the Meiji "restoration" that started Japan on the road to modernity, even mere commoners such as smiths were granted this right, and my great-grandfather Den'emon adopted the name Sakai. Thus, our family register looks something like this:

Den'emon, the smith, died in 1829.

Den'emon, the smith, died in 1839.

Den'emon Sakai, the smith, died in 1891.

After all those generations of Den'emons, it is curious that in just a single generation the adopted name of Sakai became official, and within another generation the centuries-old name of the head of our household disappeared forever. Had it not, I might well be listed as "Den'emon Sakai, the maker of companies."

Tarokichi

Kanamonoya Den'emon (Den'emon the hardware dealer) was an honest, hard-working artisan in Edo. At some point he moved his family to an area called Kanasugi, a settlement on the southeast side of the city (what is now part of Shiba, Minato-ku) at the mouth of the Kanasugi River. In time, Kanasugi would grow into a bustling commercial area, but when Den'emon moved there it was still a place of local inns, markets, and tradespeople.

Although Den'emon was blessed with three daughters, smiths need sons to work the anvil. Thus, there must have been a great celebration in the household in 1864 when a son was finally born. The boy, Tarokichi, was born just a few years before the end of the Tokugawa regime and the beginning of Japan's modern era, known as the Meiji period (1868–1912). While he was still growing up, the Shogun's rule would come to an end, Edo would be renamed Tokyo, and Japan would be catapulted into the modern world. Tarokichi was born in a feudalistic, agricultural state but grew up in a modern, industrial nation. I doubt if any country has made such a radical transition in as short a time as Japan did during the early years of the Meiji era. To be able to go back in time, to experience Tokyo during this period of transition is many a historian's dream.

Yet the end of the Shogunate and the beginning of the new Meiji era were anything but easy times for the citizens of Tokyo. Political upheaval was mirrored by social turmoil. And the "bloodless revolution" of the history books looked very different up close. The Shogunal loyalists did

Tarokichi Sakai, an extraordinarily talented inventor. Given a little more time, he would have become one of the most prominent figures in the birth of modern Japanese industry.

not give up without a fight, and their enemies, led by clans from the southern part of Japan, fought bitterly to overthrow them. These were painful years for the young nation. Important scholars who would be needed to help the nation modernize were assassinated, groups of samurai from rival factions fought often and openly, and many of the "best and brightest" young men of the time died by the sword. Even a simple artisan like Den'emon the ironsmith, who had no connection with politics, could not remain ignorant of the turmoil around him. In 1867, when Tarokichi was three years old, loyalists launched an attack on the Satsuma Mansion in Tokyo. The Satsuma clan was one of those southern families leading the movement to overthrow the Shogun and return the country to Imperial rule. Their base in Tokyo was a sizeable mansion facing the main road from Kanasugi to Shinagawa, and so close to the Sakai house that the sparks of the fire probably reached them before the news. Later that year, the Dutch legation settled on the same plot, and they, too, were burned to the ground.

In March of 1869, the city of Edo was renamed Tokyo (Eastern Capital) and the the Emperor moved from Kyoto to Tokyo, making it the official capital of the land. In the same year, a telegraph line was opened between Tokyo and Yokohama and the first lighthouses were built on promontories around Tokyo Bay. Tarokichi was five years old. In 1872 the first national school system began and elementary schools were established throughout Japan. A railroad was built between Tokyo and Yokohama, and every day thousands of people saw the gigantic, smoking symbol of the new age, a Western steam engine, racing across the landscape.

In 1875, when Tarokichi was eleven, a remarkable inventor and master craftsman came to Tokyo. Hisashige Tanaka was 78 years old when he arrived in the capital, but by all accounts he was still a bundle of energy. He opened a shop in Ginza and lived there for five years until his death, growing more famous each year for the wondrous, mechanical dolls and other devices he constructed. It is said that at the entrance of the Tanaka Workshop was a sign, "We will make any mechanism at your request." (By the way, this was the same Tanaka Workshop which would later be moved to Shibaura and eventually become Toshiba Corp.)

Tarokichi's house was only a short distance from Tanaka's shop in Ginza. Since the boy was very interested in mechanical devices, it is likely that he was one of the many who came to see Tanaka's work. Tanaka possessed a level of skill rare even among the superb craftsmen of Tokyo. I like to think that Tarokichi often visited his workshop and on occasion spoke with the master about this contraption or that. I am sure that the mechanical toys and various unfinished machines in that workshop were the subject of many a conversation between Tarokichi and his father,

Den'emon. To the teenage boy the machines were not merely evidence of a master craftsman's art, but symbols of a new civilization. Perhaps the inventive skills for which Tarokichi himself became famous were in a sense inspired by that workshop in Ginza.

Although it may seem remarkable for Tanaka to have been so creative at such an advanced age, it may be more accurate to say that his years granted him the freedom to do as he pleased. True, the ways of science and technology were just beginning to take root in this new Japan, but those who devoted themselves to such pursuits were considered highly eccentric, or in some cases, an outright burden on their families. To create anything of value inevitably required a great deal of time, tinkering, and experimentation, not something that most families could understand. Moreover, a man who would devote himself to such work, forgetting everything else and perhaps even losing his inherited land in the process, was understandably viewed as a lunatic, even a danger to his family's survival.

In this respect, Tarokichi Sakai was lucky. His father was both a craftsman and an inventor himself. He understood the joy of creation. When his young son showed both an interest and an aptitude for the same kind of things, Den'emon must have been as proud as any father in Tokyo. Rather than discourage the boy from tinkering, he taught him the secrets of metal and wood and praised him when he tried to make something new. We know from the family's oral history that the young Tarokichi developed some method for projecting the image of a machine onto a paper screen so that he could watch it operating in silhouette. Exactly how he did this is not known (he did not have electric lights to work with), but it is clear that he was already experimenting with different ways to analyze and improve the efficiency of machinery at an early age.

In August of 1887, at the age of 23, Tarokichi married a girl named Fusa. Her father had been a ricksha maker and had a workshop somewhere near Kanda. It is also said that her father was an inventor, but he died while Fusa was still young, leaving behind four children. Fusa had been attending school (the first elementary school in Tokyo), but had to quit and go look for work. For the next decade she was employed as a housemaid for a very famous architect. This gentleman, Dr. Tatsuno, later became president of the Tokyo Institute of Technology, but he is better known for the many prominent buildings he designed to adorn the new capital. Among many of his well-known buildings, the Bank of Japan and the main Tokyo Station still stand to honor his memory. It is easy to imagine that the intellectual climate in his household helped to make up for Fusa's loss of formal schooling, and it was in this lively, interesting world that she was working when she decided to marry.

When Fusa came to live with the Sakai family, she was surprised to find the closets filled with pendulum clocks and models of other machines. She was told never to straighten up these things, as they were the products of Tarokichi's imagination, and only he knew which were unfinished, which could be moved safely, and so on. She quickly realized that her husband, like her former employer Dr. Tatsuno, was no ordinary man. Indeed, young Tarokichi was a tenacious worker, and when he was inspired with an idea he became completely absorbed in it. As an idea began to take shape in his mind, he would suddenly leave the dinner table in the middle of a meal and rush into the workshop. "There he goes again," family and friends would say, shaking their heads. They thought he was more than a little eccentric, but they shrugged and left him alone.

Indeed, Tarokichi exasperated even his father with his excessive enthusiasm for tinkering with machines, but gradually the fruits of his experiments began to appear. By this time small industries were starting to spring up around Tokyo, and they needed a constant supply of tools, conveyors, machine parts and the like. The Sakai Workshop was soon producing a variety of simple, mechanical devices of a very high quality. Soon other shops around Tokyo were beginning to ask for them on a regular basis. Tarokichi the young inventor was just beginning to prove himself.

But making small mechanical parts for

Tokyo's first factories wasn't what Tarokichi had in mind. He dreamed of designing a really first-rate new machine, something that would revolutionize some industry and establish the Sakai Workshop as part of this new industrial movement. Today we might assume that he would turn his talents to something connected with steelmaking or shipbuilding. Yet these and most other fields that we think of as modern industries were still in their infancy. Instead, Tarokichi set out to revolutionize an industry that was already huge in his time and showed no signs of declining — tobacco. To understand why he chose this field to make his fame and fortune, we must understand what an important industry tobacco had become at this time.

The Golden Leaf

The custom of smoking tobacco came into Japan around 1600, probably first picked up from the Portuguese and later from the Dutch. It spread quickly among the samurai class and the well-to-do merchants. Demand grew so fast that tobacco plants were imported and planted throughout the country, from Fukushima prefecture in the north to Kyushu island in the south. In fact, so much rice land was plowed under to make room for the new crop that the Shogun's government decided to ban smoking because of the decreasing acreage of farm

Tobacco-smoking, if not the first custom imported from the West, was certainly the most popular. The smoking of pipe tobacco had become a major fashion by the 19th century and was also a hugely profitable industry.

land. Ultimately a "pipe hunt" (a reminder of the old "sword hunt") was carried out in Edo to try to stamp out the practice, but with little success. What really guaranteed the spread of tobacco, however, was the government's poor fiscal management. In 1725, with its finances in a shambles, the central government decided it was time to profit from the people's vice rather than trying to eliminate it. In other words, they legalized tobacco, and began taxing it as a commodity.

Several areas of the country were designated as authorized tobacco production centers, and the foreign leaf flourished. Records show that by 1840 these centers were shipping over 4,000 tons of tobacco to Edo every year. In the capital, men of means carried elaborately carved gold and silver pipes, and tobacco pouches made of imported cloth were hung with coral *netsuke* ornaments (now collectors' items), as smokers became ever more fashion-conscious.

By Tarokichi's day the production and sale of pipe tobacco was a huge industry. Yet this industry relied on a single inefficient device to reap its profits: the tobacco shredder. Seldom more than a crude wooden frame with a straight metal blade used to chop layers of pressed tobacco leaves, the shredders of the day were little more than short mechanical guillotines. The result was very coarse tobacco of uneven widths that looked hacked rather than finely sliced. What the tobacco industry needed was an efficient machine that would automatically advance a stack of pressed leaves at a constant speed towards a razor-sharp blade that would consistently slice them as thin as possible.

Tarokichi saw one of the old machines and knew immediately that he could make a better one. If even a few of the tobacco companies adopted his design, the Sakai Workshop would have orders for years to come. So he and Den'emon set about building a precision tobacco shredder. It took them some time to devise exactly the right mechanism, but by combining the son's ingenuity with the father's mastery of machinery, they created something much better than either had dared to hope for. The Sakai Tobacco Shredder was an engineering marvel. It had a smooth-running engine that advanced even layers of pressed tobacco leaves, moving them at just the right speed into a vertical blade assembly where they could be cut to a uniform fineness unimaginable at the time. It was exactly what the private tobacco firms were looking for.

Sadly, Den'emon would never enjoy the tremendous success that was soon to result from his and his son's labors. He died in 1891, just as the family business was beginning to take off. Tarokichi was 27 and Fusa 22. Their first son, Kan'ichi, was born a week after Den'emon's death.

As Tarokichi had planned, the quality of his design was enough to insure that its reputation would spread, and the Sakai Workshop could probably have done a good business just selling equipment to the private tobacco companies. But Fate seemed to have marked the little company for another kind of success altogether.

In 1894 Japan went to war against China. As part of its efforts to raise the necessary funds to finance the war, the government decided to nationalize the tobacco business. It established a Monopoly Corporation which took over the private firms cultivating and selling tobacco. In the process, it became apparent that the tobacco from different shops was of very uneven quality, which made it difficult to sort and grade. The Monopoly Corporation then decided to take over the whole business. Since the shredding equipment was the key to improved production quality, they held a national competition to determine the ideal shredding machine with which to standardize the production process.

The Sakai machine that was entered in the competition was a tribute to Tarokichi's and Den'emon's craftsmanship. The frame was made of extremely hard zelkova wood brought in from the countryside near Mt. Fuji. Each log was carefully cut so that the reddish core would become the center of each board, making it even more durable. The device had four different gear ratios with which the operator could adjust the movement of the tobacco leaves and the width of the shredding. The blade was slightly curved, like a Japanese sword, and cut perfectly, producing tobacco so fine you would swear it was spun like a thread rather than cut from a leaf. The machine won the competition easily and was declared the new government standard for use throughout the country.

I had always heard about the precision cutting of this old Sakai machine, but oddly enough, it was the writings of a foreigner that piqued my interest in seeing it work. Perhaps you have heard of Lafcadio Hearn (1850–1904), an American who came to Japan in 1890 as a magazine correspondent. He chose to stay on in Japan rather than to return home, married a local woman, Setsuko Koizumi (hence the adopted name by which he is known in Japan, Yakumo Koizumi), and obtained Japanese citizenship. Hearn taught English at two top universities and wrote several books on the customs and lifestyles of old Japan. I am not the person to ask about the extent of his literary skills, but I can say that as a foreign reporter looking at the world around him, his essays provide some interesting insights into Japanese society at the turn of the century.

In one such essay Hearn talks about the habit of smoking among Japanese of his day, especially the elegant pipes and tobacco pouches that were so common. He describes how a gentleman picks the shredded tobacco from his pouch with his fingertips and places it carefully in the bowl of his pipe. Most remarkable to me, the extremely fine strands of tobacco lead Hearn to compare it to the softness of a woman's hair. While the image may seem quite poetic, I always suspected Hearn of

The author with one of the original Sakai tobacco shredders, in use for more than 80 years.

overstepping the bounds of literary license. How could a wooden-framed device that was built and operated by hand a hundred years ago—even one designed by my own grandfather—slice anything with that degree of precision?

Then in May of 1980, the Salt and Tobacco Museum in Tokyo announced a display and demonstration of the Sakai tobacco shredder. What a wonderful opportunity, I thought, to take my own son to see these old machines and for both of us to examine the skills of our ancestors. At the museum I noticed that not only the general public, but engineers from several top Japanese manufacturers had come to see the machine in action. And they, like myself, stood shaking their heads in disbelief. The machine on display dated from 1910, but it ran as smoothly and cut as perfectly as if Tarokichi had just oiled it a few minutes before the demonstration. And to all of our amazement, the tobacco was cut so fine that it truly looked like soft, reddish-brown hair. In fact, museum records show the exact widths specified for different grades of tobacco, and one of the highest grades requires a fineness of approximately 0.1 millimeter, just about the thickness of a human hair. Clearly, Mr. Hearn was not exaggerating.

Was Tarokichi's design merely a good piece of work considering the limits of nineteenth century technology? Far from it. This same basic design from the 1890s was used with little modification for almost a century. The Sakai-type shredder was formally retired only in 1979—not because it had been replaced by anything more precise or more reliable, but because its product— shredded tobacco—was no longer sold. For more than eighty years, though, every pouch of pipe tobacco made in Japan was produced using Tarokichi's device, and every machine of his design bore the stamp "Sakai" on its side.

But let's go back to the dimly lit Sakai Workshop, to the days just before the Monopoly Corporation's competition. In those days, indoor lighting was done almost exclusively with kerosene lamps. The light was weak, but at least it was better than the old paper-covered oil lamps used in Japan for centuries. Of course there were electric lights in the streets of Ginza, but not in most people's homes. Besides, the electric lights had thin bamboo filaments which made them even weaker than kerosene. Consequently, kerosene lamps were very common—and so were fires. Until World War II, Tokyo was a city made largely of wood and paper, and with so many lamps and cooking fires lit at night, the odds were good that the next major conflagration was just around the corner. From ancient times fires were called one of the "flowers of Edo," something people came to accept as part of city life.

In mid-December of 1895 a fire broke out one afternoon in Kanasugi. It was a small one by Tokyo standards (only 157 houses and six temples were consumed), but it was big enough to reduce both the Sakai Workshop and the family home to ashes. December is the most hectic time for businesses in Japan (tradition says that all accounts must be settled and books closed by the end of the month). To lose both one's business and family house before the New Year's celebration is about as great a blow as could befall a man. Moreover, when we consider how many of Tarokichi's half-finished projects went up in smoke that day, the loss is doubly painful.

But Tarokichi was young and determined. He immediately set about rebuilding everything from scratch. First he built a small home for his family, then began construction of a new, bigger factory. It would be a brick building this time (quite a new idea in those days), and he vowed that this new factory would withstand any fire that swept the neighborhood. I have always suspected that his wife Fusa, having spent many years in the home of one of Japan's top architects, had some say in this decision and perhaps even in the actual planning. In any case, like everything Tarokichi built, the new building was made to last. It not only withstood the Tokyo earthquake of 1927 that levelled much of the city, but even the repeated bombings of 1945. It is still standing today, weathered but proud, a tribute to a man's vision almost a century ago.

Predictably, Tarokichi devoted all his energies in the winter of 1896 to rebuilding his home and his factory. He worked from early morning until midnight every day without a break, using up energy that he would soon need to fight for his own life. For shortly after fire ravaged the neighborhood, typhoid fever followed, cutting through the district like a scythe. Soon enough, the exhausted Tarokichi fell ill and was taken to a clinic. But in those days, to be hospitalized usually meant that death would soon follow.

Tarokichi died in the middle of 1896, at the age of 32. I wince at the thought of the anguish he must have suffered, lying helplessly in bed with his factory half-built, dozens of new inventions swirling in his head, and his pretty young wife pregnant with their third son.

The only bright spot was that the Tobacco Monopoly Corporation had announced the results of their competition. Thus, before he died Tarokichi knew that one of his machines had been tested against rivals from all over Japan and judged to be the best. It must have seemed small consolation, but it was all he had.

Tarokichi Sakai was my grandfather. His unborn son was later named Naokichi, perhaps a reminder of the father whose face he never saw and whose love he never knew. This was my father, Naokichi Sakai. When I was young, I used to ask him about my grandfather. He would pause for a moment. His voice would soften to an almost reverential tone, his face would brighten, he would smile and say, "Your grandpa was a wonderful man who invented wonderful machines. He was truly a great man." People said that among Taro- kichi's three sons it was Naokichi who most resembled his father. If that is accurate, Tarokichi must indeed have been a remarkable man.

A Woman's Sacrifice

When Tarokichi died so suddenly, he left behind two legacies, a successful business and a resourceful young wife. The business, despite the temporary setback of the fire, was soon going well. Once the Sakai machine had proved itself, the Monopoly Corporation began a steady flow of orders that kept the small workshop busy day and night. When government demand finally exceeded the small shop's ability to build the units to spe- cification, the Corporation allowed some parts to be produced at other shops, what today we would call subcontracting. In such cases, men from the Sakai workshop had to be present at the sub- contractors to examine their work. They were even paid as inspectors by the Monopoly Cor- poration. Eventually, the machines were shipped as far away as Korea and Taiwan, and Sakai company employees had to travel abroad to in- struct the users in their proper care and operation. In short, the business Tarokichi left behind was in very good shape. '

The young wife was in a much more difficult

Fusa Sakai, Tarokichi's wife and Naokichi's mother. A loyal, strong-willed woman, she would not allow her husband's work and her children's inheritance to be stolen by jealous relatives.

position. Fusa was all of twenty-seven years old, had two sons (Kan'ichi was six and Taro three), and was pregnant with Naokichi. You might think that at least she was in the enviable position of inheriting a growing business, yet because of her youth and the fact that she was a woman in a strongly male-dominated society, things were not so simple.

It is sad but true that when a dead man's relatives begin to express their opinions about the future disposition of his estate, they are often suspected of being motivated more by self-interest than by concern for the dear departed. This is an unfortunate but perhaps natural assumption, and in the case of Tarokichi's relatives, completely justified.

"Running a growing factory would be a tremendous burden for such a young widow," they said. "And think of the poor children with no father at home and a mother all caught up in the day-to-day affairs of running a business. Why don't we help out by managing the business so that Tarokichi's work can continue smoothly?" In particular, Tarokichi's three sisters (and their husbands) were insistent that the business should be kept "in the family." The obvious implication was that Fusa was part of Tarokichi's family but not of theirs. With him gone, their blood relationship counted more than any contract between husband and wife.

Perhaps the sisters thought that it would be

fairly easy to take the business away from a silly young girl with no one to help her. If so, they should have known better. For Tarokichi was a man who did everything carefully. He was a perfectionist. He would not have married a silly, frivolous girl any more than he would have used inferior tools to create his inventions. Moreover, he had great plans for his business and needed a wife who would not merely support him but help him to bring his dreams to fruition. Undoubtedly, Tarokichi married wisely, though his sisters might not have thought so at first. Fusa was still young, but she was also bright, strong-willed, and extremely protective of her family. She knew that if the management of Tarokichi's business were to pass over to the sisters' husbands, she and her children would soon become an awkward reminder that the business wasn't theirs to begin with. The children would only be more in the way with each passing year, and one way or another, their inheritance would be stolen. She resolved to stand her ground, even to fight for her sons' rights if necessary.

Realizing that she could not do this alone, she finally went for help to a neighborhood counsellor, a man named Itokawa who was reputed to be wise in legal matters. She explained the situation to him in detail. He told her to appoint her eldest son Kan'ichi as successor to the business under the guardianship of an experienced employee at the shop who had worked closely with

Tarokichi. Then, to formalize the arrangement, she must establish a new "family" using the Sakai name. That is, she must set up a branch of the family separate from the three sisters and to formalize it she must marry the guardian and make him the head of the new Sakai line. Only in this way could she secure the inheritance under Japanese civil law. (It may be interesting to note that this type of marriage, in which a man marries the female head of a family and assumes her name and position, remained fairly common and was only eliminated from civil law in 1947.)

Fusa understood the importance of Itokawa's advice, but for obvious reasons could not imagine marrying again. As time went by, however, and the relatives' intentions became more overt, she began increasingly to fear for her children. Gradually she realized that this disagreeable plan was the only way to keep the Sakai factory safe for her children to inherit. Thus, she finally agreed to marry Tarokichi's favorite apprentice, a young man named Watanabe, several years her junior. He agreed to the plan, and they were married in a simple ceremony at a noodle restaurant near the Sakai home.

Watanabe, the young apprentice turned master, was also in a difficult position. At age twenty-one he was not only married with two stepsons, but also in charge of a going concern and guardian of its legal heir. Three months after his marriage to Fusa, Naokichi was born, which made three of Tarokichi's children that he had to look after. Watanabe (for clarity's sake, I shall continue to call him that, although his legal name was now Sakai) was a young man thrust into a situation he could never have anticipated.

There is no doubt that he was both faithful to Fusa and loyal to the heir, her eldest son, Kan'ichi, all his life. Whatever else we may say about him, Watanabe carried out his part of the bargain. He was also ingenious, hardworking and helped to insure that Tarokichi's inventions came into wide use. On the pamphlets that went with each shredding machine he printed Tarokichi's name and on the plates of the machines he inscribed Kan'ichi's name. We cannot accuse him of faithlessness nor of self-aggrandizement at the family's expense.

Yet he seemed to take the arrangement to provide for Fusa and Kan'ichi quite literally. He felt a lifelong obligation towards the two of them, as was the intent of his marriage. But he seemed to feel no special warmth for the rest of the family. The second son, Taro, was never treated as well as Kan'ichi, and the third son, Naokichi (who of course came along after the marriage was arranged), was treated as an unwanted pest. Can we, or should we blame Watanabe for his callousness towards the other children? This is not a question I can easily answer. But the fact remains that Naokichi had a miserable childhood.

Naokichi

Shortly after Naokichi was born, his step-father put him out to nurse at a neighbor's home. Fusa scarcely had a chance to hold him in her arms, but reconciled herself to the situation as part of her obligation to her new husband. She was also very busy in those days. Among other things, she had to make clothing and prepare meals for the workers in the shop—and that may be one reason why she yielded to the decision to send her baby to another household. With Fusa's waking hours already fully occupied, and two other children crying for attention, Naokichi would seldom have had a mother to watch over him anyway. And yet, Fusa was a woman of strong emotion, and the decision to send him away for over two years must have hurt her deeply.

At the age of three Naokichi came back home, but not for long. This time he was sent as a servant to a local charcoal merchant. It may seem unthinkable to us for a child of three to be working at a stranger's home, especially when his family was not in any financial difficulty, but by this time Watanabe had produced two children of his own, making Naokichi even more of a nuisance. Fusa may have thought it better to send the boy away than to see him mistreated at home.

In the old days, charcoal was the only fuel for cooking and heating, and the local charcoal-seller was a familiar face in the neighborhood. When he was finished cutting charcoal, small chips and pieces too small to burn would be left over. These pieces were put into a rectangular hopper with a fine mesh on the bottom which hung suspended by ropes. By swinging it back and forth vigorously to sift out the charcoal dust, then mixing the dust with a kind of glue, it was possible to make charcoal balls big enough to sell. Through this process no gram of charcoal was wasted.

At the age of three Naokichi's job was to sit on the ground by this hanging sieve and swing the rope back and forth all day shaking out charcoal dust. Because the work was especially dirty, he was placed at the front of the charcoal-seller's open shop, and passersby would often remark at the little boy covered with soot from head to toe, working so diligently to make charcoal balls.

Years went by before Naokichi was able to leave the charcoal-seller and return to his own family, but even then he was ridiculed by his older brothers. "Hey, don't forget you're the charcoal man's kid," they taunted, "You're the grubby little thing who used to sit in front of that dirty shop, covered in soot, pulling on that stupid rope all day! You're really the pride of the Sakai household, let me tell you!" Even when he began to help out in the family Workshop, he was treated as little more than a lower-class worker.

In Japan we often say that to coddle a child will make him self-centered, and there are many sayings to the effect that the pampered child does not understand suffering: "One who knows not the taste of his own tears cannot feel the pains of another." A good case in point was Naokichi's eldest brother, Kan'ichi, the young heir for whom his mother had sacrificed so much. He was badly spoiled and turned out to be a nasty child and, later, a totally unremarkable man.

There is another saying, "Leave the child alone and let him grow by himself," indicating that a good parent need not interfere much in his child's early life. There is even a sense that the deprived child will grow straight and true. Naokichi was perhaps a good example of this philosophy. Although his boyhood was hard and painful, he grew to be a man of firm character, with a sound, compassionate heart. How could a young man survive in such a cold world and even turn out to have a warm heart of his own? The secret lies in the one source of warmth that never wavered throughout his life: his mother's affection. Even when she was persuaded to send Naokichi to a neighbor's home for long periods of time or had to watch him suffer as a lowly employee in his father's own shop, Fusa felt for her child. Perhaps she had a special fondness for him because he was her last child by Tarokichi, the last thing he created before his death. As an old man, Naokichi used to remember, "My mother would mix buckwheat flour and hot water into a mash for me," and his eyes would take on a dreamy look, as if he was seeing something or someone very far away, "The way she made that mash for me, sometimes late at night after the family had gone to bed... There was nothing better in the whole world." I wonder if the way his mother's hot buckwheat warmed him on a cold night reminded him of the warmth she always felt for him despite the cold world around him.

Naokichi's boyhood was a simple routine. He slept in the servants' quarters and ate his meals at a small table apart from the other children. At 6 am he awoke and went to the factory where he worked from 7 am until 9 pm with a half hour off for lunch. In those days, of course, there was no such thing as a five-day week, or even a six-day week. The 1st and the 15th of each month were given as workers' holidays, but all other days were regular work days. As he got a bit older, Naokichi was able to enroll in a special nighttime elementary school for working children, which meant he could leave work at 5 pm to go to school.

Unlike his brothers, Naokichi loved school and worked very hard. His sufferings at home made him all the more intent to study hard and do well in school. For school was the one place he was treated fairly and where his abilities were recognized. He not only studied hard at the elementary school, but attended an English-language school every evening as well. Two years later when he graduated from Shiba Elementary School, he was proclaimed one of the best students the school had ever had. The boy was elated but his father and siblings were furious to see their little "shop boy" doing well in the outside world.

From Shiba Elementary, he passed the entrance examination for a trade school attached to the School of Technology (the predecessor of the Tokyo Institute of Technology). He studied there for one year, then asked his stepfather for permission to enter the famous Municipal School of Industrial Arts in Tsukiji. His stepfather refused out of hand. How could such a worthless child hope for an advanced education? Moreover, for the kind of work he would be doing in the factory, it was unnecessary. Absolutely out of the question, his stepfather said.

Naokichi was crushed. His other brothers and even half-brothers had all received higher education, although none of them showed the least aptitude for it (Kan'ichi needed to repeat one year of high school three times before being admitted to prestigious Waseda University). Naokichi wanted to go to the Municipal School of Industrial Arts more than anything he had ever wanted, and his mother knew it. Fusa pleaded with her husband repeatedly, and finally he relented. "If you want to study that much, go ahead and take the entrance exam," he agreed. "But only once. If you fail, you will give up these foolish ideas and return to your work full-time."

Watanabe must have known that Naokichi was not qualified even to sit for the exam at this famous school, much less be able to pass it. The first hurdle was not so difficult, however. While the boy did not have the required number of years of study, the school administration took into account his hard work at night school, and allowed him to sit for the exam anyway. It was a noble but futile effort. Naokichi's only study of formal subjects such as Chemistry and Japanese composition had been from reading old textbooks that his brothers had thrown away. There was no way he could pass a test on such topics. And he didn't. He failed most sections of the test. Which meant that his one shot to get into the school and away from home had also failed. He was miserable.

Then, Fate seems to have played a hand. Despite the boy's poor showing in most subjects, the examiners were impressed by his superb performance in mathematics and his fierce desire to study. They decided that he had tremendous potential, and so admitted him in spite of his low test scores. Years later he confided, "I tried with all my heart to get into that school because I knew that if I failed I would be a lowly workman in my stepfather's shop forever. It is only by the grace of God that I was admitted."

His first year at the school was even more difficult. Again, many of the subjects were new and confusing to him. He found it impossible keep up with the other boys. Naokichi's answer was to study twice as hard. By his second year he was getting high marks, and by his third year his teachers were saying he was the best student in the school's history. He received a scholarship which paid all his tuition until graduation.

School life was not easy, but it provided a great relief from his home life. Upon entering the school, his stepfather made him promise to work at the factory every day after classes, and this he did faithfully. Every morning for four years he rose at six in the morning, oiled all the machinery in the plant, walked some distance to school, then hurried home immediately afterwards, put on a workman's uniform, and worked until 7 pm. After dinner, he studied until ten o'clock. There is no doubt that he was naturally a good student. But there was also the fear that at any moment his stepfather might change his mind and he might lose the opportunity to study forever.

Naokichi's success at school irked both his stepfather and his brothers and they did not hesitate to show it. They enjoyed coming up with annoying errands for him to do on the way to school—go visit this customer, collect money from that one, and buy some materials for the shop when you are finished. The boy did each one without complaint, but this only enraged them more and made them search for new ways to torment him.

Naokichi's favorite subject at school was drafting. This was perhaps natural, since like his father he was a quiet, methodical boy who was especially gifted in mechanical things. He stood head and shoulders above his peers when it came to drafting and was proud of his achievements. After work was finished he would sit up late at night with rulers and a compass, doing each assignment with meticulous care, sometimes spending many nights on a single project. Once, after working for many nights on an especially difficult project, he awoke to find his completed drawing torn to shreds. In a panic, he cried out "Who ripped up my work?" The door opened and his stepfather looked in. "I did. What about it?" It took all of his effort to keep his anger and his tears bottled up inside. On other occasions his brothers spilled ink on his drawings, but still he said nothing. He knew that if he were seen to be quarrelling with his brothers his stepfather would use it as an excuse and order him to quit school immediately.

At the end of his four years at the School of Industrial Arts, Naokichi had to confront his stepfather once more. Having come this far, he wanted nothing more than to complete his education at a top university. He dreamed of going to Waseda, one of the best private schools in Japan, and when one of his teachers said, "You'll do well there. I'd be glad to write a letter of recommendation," he was determined to get into the university.

His stepfather and Kan'ichi both objected strongly. "What's a bumpkin like you going to do at a fine university? You're a charcoal-seller's lackey who's lucky to be working in a respectable machine shop. Stop putting on airs. The education you've had is already more than you'll ever need."

But Naokichi would not give up. He pleaded and begged, and his mother also begged her husband to let the boy enter Waseda. Finally, in a rage, he shouted, "If you insist on going to the damn university, fine! But from this day forward don't show your face in this house. You will have no rights here. You'll forfeit your inheritance! You'll get nothing, not a penny! Agreed?"

Naokichi did not hesitate. His "inheritance" in this household meant only more suffering, while a university education might mean a world of new opportunity. He would go. In April of 1916, at the age of twenty, Naokichi entered the preparatory course for Waseda University. His major was mechanical engineering. Having been a scholarship student at the School of Industrial Arts, he was admitted without examination.

I have seen photos of his school days, and they speak of a relaxed, even happy young man beginning to free himself at last from his family and enjoy life on his own. One of his lifelong passions was kabuki, a form of traditional Japanese drama. Even while still attending the School of Industrial Arts he managed to steal away occasionally and go to the Kabuki-za theater. After entering university, he had a little more time to himself and went to see the classical plays whenever he could. He loved to stand in the gallery and memorize the repertoire of the great

Ginza at the beginning of the 20th century, a cultural crossroads in the new Japan. Tarokichi and Naokichi lived not far away and both visited here often. Today Ginza is home to the headquarters of the Bunsha Group.

actors. He learned not only the plots of the major plays, but the lineages of all the prominent performers. After the war, when the Kabuki-za had not yet been rebuilt, he used to go to the Tohgeki Theater to see the kabuki. There were only two or three rows of hard benches in the gallery, but the real fans would crowd in there, calling out the names of the actors at the climax of each performance. "In the kabuki drama we can see the essence of Japanese tradition," Naokichi would sometimes say. "And we can understand the sufferings of common people." I am sure there was something more than literary appreciation in his love of this drama.

The Growth of Industry

Japan only started on its path to modernization in the 1870s, so by the turn of the century Japanese industry was still in its infancy. England's industrial revolution was more than a century old while even a latecomer like the United States had been industrializing for decades. They were world leaders in almost every form of science and technology while Japan was still trying to get started. However, since the beginning of the Meiji period the Japanese government had been sending some of its best and brightest young men abroad to study Western science. In this way, developments in other countries were regularly reported back to Tokyo where the most promising among them could be duplicated.

In the Sakai Factory, for example, it was very apparent that every time the machines were started up the gears would rattle and buzz, a sign of imperfect manufacturing. In America and Europe precision-made gears were already being produced on special milling machines, but such equipment was as yet unknown in Japan. Gradually, through its industry-watchers overseas, the government became aware of the superiority of such uniform gears and their importance to the development of modern industry. As a result, the Monopoly Corporation changed its order specifications to require milled-gear machines. This strategy is worth noting. With limited funds available, the national government did not set out to build prototypes of new machines and then recommend them to industry, which would have been costly and time-consuming. Instead, it simply required their use in the manufacture of products already under contract. Of course, the Sakai Factory was by this time already one of the nation's most advanced machinery plants, and thus a good lab" in which to test the equipment at no cost to the government. The Sakai Factory then had to make the investment, learn how to use the new machines, and apply the imported technology as quickly as possible. Which is just what they did. The firm ordered a universal milling machine from a company in New Jersey and set about translating the instruction manuals into Japanese. By this time young Naokichi was well versed in English, and so provided both the linguistic and mechanical skills necessary to set up and run the machinery properly. Thus, Japan's first gear manufacturing plant came to be established.

The truly astounding feature of this equipment was that it worked by itself, not just for an hour or two, but for days on end. Once everything was set and adjusted properly, the machine milled its gears automatically for three days without any need for human workers to intervene. Even while the factory slept, the machinery kept on working. This seemed a miracle at the time. No one had ever heard of such a concept as "automation," but in fact the Sakai Factory was the only shop in Japan to have put automation to use. It was the beginning of industrial automation in Japan, and a forerunner of today's giant factories run entirely by robots.

In fact, the use of such machinery was such a radical step for Japanese industry that a prominent magazine wrote a long article describing this new technology. That piece alerted other manufacturers to the existence of such equipment and its implementation on Japanese soil, and served as a tremendous advertisement for the Sakai business. In no time at all the firm was besieged by visitors and flooded with orders to make all sorts of machinery. From the quality and reliability of Tarokichi's tobacco shredder had come a government mandate to acquire and implement the newest in Western technology, and from that had come national recognition as a leader in mechanical engineering. The Sakai Ironworks, as the firm was now known, had suddenly become enormously profitable.

Unfortunately, the little family firm had no concept of how to function as a corporation. They were simple workmen, some extremely talented to be sure, but none an accountant, a manager, or an executive. Their strength was in creating not in managing, and their incompetence kept the firm from growing as it should have in light of its very sizeable profits.

First, Watanabe retired. Though only in his forties, he could now well afford to leave the company and retire to a life of comfort. He built a substantial home in another part of Tokyo, hired several gardeners, and had the house remodelled several times. He also began to indulge in the pleasures of the rich. He had a passion for hunting. He even kept hounds and hired helpers to join in their regular outings. Gradually the old man grew too fat to hunt and took up shooting birds instead. When he grew too fat for that, he switched to fishing. One thing was missing from his new house, however. Fusa did not go with him, but stayed behind to take care of the workers and apprentices at the factory. She cooked for them and washed their uniforms. Perhaps it was loyalty to the men, perhaps she simply didn't want to leave the factory where her husband had once worked and for which she had made such sacrifices to keep it out of the hands of his jealous siblings.

Kan'ichi, who had by now married, assumed the leadership of the family. Yet he was even less suited to manage than his stepfather had been. Because the firm now had a monopoly on an important new technology, he became openly arrogant and contemptuous of his clients. He and his wife used to say to anyone who would listen, "We aren't like you common people. We belong to a different class." Fusa would cringe to hear her own son talking this way.

When Naokichi graduated from Waseda, it was a whole new world in which he found himself. He did not even have a chance to start again at the Sakai Ironworks, for he was immediately called into military service. The First World War had just ended, and the government considered it an object lesson in the importance of having a strong military. Naokichi was assigned to an elite squadron of army engineers who serviced the fledgling air corps. Japan had obtained, among other craft, several monoplanes, but had no manuals to explain their equipment. It thus fell to Naokichi to analyze their engines, find out what they required, and keep them running at peak performance. Emergency landings were all too common in those days, and Naokichi, an amateur photographer, took many photos of planes lying upside-down or standing on end, some with their wings shorn off. Looking at the materials and the workmanship in some of those planes, he realized they were really little more than complex kites, but it was his duty to keep them flying, and he did that very well. Before he left the military he found himself promoted. He entered the service as a conscript and left as an officer.

When he finished his military service, he returned to the family business. A year later, around noon on September 1, 1923 he was working inside the factory in Kanasugi when the building began to shake. There was an awful cracking sound and Naokichi looked up just in time to see a solid 12-inch thick wooden beam snap like a toothpick. But it wasn't just their building—the roof of a factory up the street collapsed and buildings up and down the block were caving in. It was several minutes before the ground stopped shaking.

This was the Great Kanto Earthquake, which levelled much of the city and killed tens of thousands. Somehow, the Sakai Ironworks was spared. Decades before, Tarokichi had built his factory out of brick to be sure it would be fireproof. But it was more than fireproof; it was solid. It remained standing despite internal damage, and stood alone when other brick buildings were destroyed. Even the machines inside were still running, but when the ground finally stopped moving, a quick look at the workers' faces told Naokichi that their thoughts were all on their

Survivors of the Great Kanto Earthquake of 1923 flee the ruins of Tokyo. Thousands of buildings were levelled (though Tarokichi's factory survived), fires ravaged the city and the death toll was in the tens of thousands.

families' safety. He closed the factory and told them to get on home. Then, the streetcars having stopped, he walked home.

During the night fires began to spread from one part of the city to another, and in due course they engulfed Kanasugi. People in the neighborhood, seeing the Sakai Ironworks factory still standing and remembering Tarokichi's vow that it would withstand any blaze, rushed to put their household possessions inside for safekeeping. Unfortunately, the building worked like an oven; the outer brick walls heated up, and everything inside, from the neighbors' clothing to the company's machinery, was completely consumed.

The first night back, Naokichi saw the damage. He slept outside by the still warm factory walls, then began the next day to salvage and repair the machinery. It took him the best part of a year to get things back to normal again, and he had to work like a slave to do it, just as his father had done years before when another fire had destroyed his own factory. Was Kan'ichi grateful? Did he begin to treat his younger brother with more respect and friendship? Not in the slightest.

Naokichi knew it was time to leave the family business.

He heard there was an opening for an engineer at one of Tokyo's two main bus companies. He had to ask permission from Watanabe to apply for the job, and his stepfather was just as encouraging and supportive as always: "Go ahead, take the job. You won't amount to much outside of this factory, but go see if the bus company is dumb enough to take you on."

Not only was Naokichi hired, he was promoted to chief engineer on the same day. This is probably an indication of how rare it was to have a graduate from a top university seek a job in common industry. The chief engineer's duty was to maintain the engines and drive trains of the bus fleet and be sure they would all pass a government inspection every six months. This might not seem like much of a challenge today, but at the time buses were so shaky that it was quite common for the drive shaft to drop off or the gear shift to slip out while the bus was in motion. Naokichi had his work cut out for him.

After months of rebuilding and maintaining the buses under his direction, the inspection day came. But when the chief inspector walked into the office he turned out to be an old friend of Naokichi's from Waseda. "I know your work, Naokichi. There's no point in wasting my time looking at these engines," he said and handed over the inspection stamp on the spot. Everyone knew they'd hired the right man for the job.

He stayed at the bus company for some years, but was never really happy there. In retrospect, the job seems to have been more a way to get away from Kan'ichi. But the bus company proved to be an important education for Naokichi in another way. It was there that he discovered how people in big companies tend to be lazy, incompetent, or worse. Some, he noted, collected their monthly paycheck without doing any work and felt no sense of shame. After all, it was a big company, right?

This attitude was something unknown back at the Sakai factory, where workers were treated more like family and there wasn't even the opportunity for slacking off. For the rest of his life Naokichi would refer back to his experience at the bus company as his first glimpse of how bad the attitudes of workers at big companies can be. And he passed on to his own son a profound distaste for "big company disease".

An Interesting Neighbor

Allow me to digress just for a moment to introduce a merchant family named Kobayashi who lived just down the street from the Sakai plant. Mr. Kobayashi was a very shrewd businessman and stories of his younger days were legendary in the neighborhood. Years earlier he had run a large inn with many customers coming and going. This proved to be an ideal way to conceal his 'other' business, making illegal sake. Once, the police raided the inn in search of evidence just after Kobayashi's wife had finished entering their accounts in a secret ledger. As the police barged into the house, she deftly shoved the ledger into a pot of cooked rice and welcomed them to search as they liked. They found nothing, and went on their way. Later on, Kobayashi was finally caught, but was acquitted by a judge who happened to come from a sake-brewing family. Upon his release, Kobayashi was offered membership in the brewer's union, but turned it down. He hadn't given up making sake; he just didn't want to do it legally.

He purchased a house on the main street in Kanasugi just a stone's throw from the Sakai residence and opened a store selling *miso* (a soy paste almost as much of a staple in Japanese cuisine as rice). His business was very successful, and he later invested in a variety of ventures, including stage and movie theaters.

The Kobayashis had four sons, but the star of the family was their second daughter, Kiyoe. When she was very young Kiyoe would come home from elementary school every day to help measure out the miso for customers. Being a naturally good-natured girl, it was her custom to be generous with portions (a most uncharacteristic habit among merchants). When she put a little too much miso on the scale, she would simply hand it over, saying "Thank you very much" and beam her winning smile. Her father soon heard from happy customers how his daughter was giving away a little extra with each sale. Most merchant fathers would have scolded their child severely for giving away house profits, but Kobayashi was a smart businessman. He knew this was the best kind of

Kiyoe Kobayashi with her mother. Even as a child, the "star" of the Kobayashi family was famous for her generosity, but her most important role was as Naokichi's wife and Kuniyasu's mother.

advertising and decided to let Kiyoe handle all the
sales work by herself after school. The Kobayashi
shop was soon bustling with customers. A newspaper story featuring a photo of Kiyoe only added
to the publicity. At New Year's, Kiyoe would give
away free miso to jobless people in the neighborhood. In no time at all, the store's reputation had
spread and the Kobayashi family prospered.

As Kiyoe grew, the family came to depend
on her more and more. She learned to do the store
accounts on an abacus like a pro and gradually took
over much of the family's bookkeeping. One autumn morning in 1923, when she was eighteen,
Kiyoe was told to withdraw all the family's funds
from their usual bank and deposit them in the
Kangyo Bank (later to become the Dai-Ichi Kangyo Bank). Kiyoe set off to the bank, withdrew
what must have been a very large sum of cash,
wrapped it in a large cloth bundle, and started
walking to the Kangyo Bank. Just before noon she
was almost knocked to the ground—it seemed as
if all of Tokyo was being shaken like the branch of
a tree. She knew this was no ordinary Tokyo
tremor, but a massive earthquake. As roofs collapsed and fires broke out around the city, Kiyoe
realized that even if the Kangyo Bank was still
standing it would be impossible to get into. All the
banks would have to close immediately or face a
"run" by their depositors. So as soon as the ground
stopped shaking, she shoved the bundle of cash
inside her kimono and made her way home.

Thanks to her presence of mind—and her extreme good fortune to have just withdrawn all all her family's funds—the Kobayashi family was rescued. At a time when the financial world was in chaos, credit nonexistent, and all sales being made in cash, Kiyoe returned home safe and sound carrying all the family's assets inside her kimono.

As we saw earlier at the Sakai factory, destruction continued for days after the Great Earthquake. Fires raged through the city, disease spread, and bodies were stacked up on street corners. Homes that were not flattened were razed by the flames. Kobayashi emptied out his store and took his family to shelter further south in the city. Then, with the money that Kiyoe had rescued, he headed back to his hometown in the countryside. There he bought out the contents of a large hardware store and purchased all the lumber he could find. While people were still streaming out of the devastated capital, a line of trucks carrying Kobayashi's goods was rolling into the city. He set up shop in a vacant lot near Shiba Park and sold everything that people would need to rebuild their homes and their lives. Along with the lumber, he brought three dozen carpenters to build a permanent store for this business. As soon as they were finished, he ordered more lumber and had them create a "prefab" 2-room house. This small but solid unit was exactly what was needed by hundreds of families whose dwellings had been demolished. The carpenters set up a kind of "assembly line" production and in no time at all Kobayashi had sold 500 houses. With the profits he rented several more vacant lots and told the carpenters to build houses for rent. Soon he had rented more than 500 of these units and had become an important landlord. (It might be interesting to note that had he bought the land instead of renting it, his descendents today would all be billionaires).

As life settled back to normal in Tokyo, the Kobayashi family returned to the store just up the street from the Sakai Ironworks, and their prosperity continued to grow.

A New Life

In 1927, at the age of thirty-two, Naokichi did a remarkable thing: He began dating a girl.

Until that time his life had been solely taken up with work, study, and more work. Girls and social life were not even on the menu. But one day an acquaintance suggested a formal meeting with a girl of good family who lived just down the street. Kiyoe Kobayashi must have known of Naokichi, the neighborhood "genius," but it seems they had never met formally.

Fortunately, Naokichi had the good sense to realize that there was more to life than being an engineer for a bus company, and agreed to the meeting. In 1927 proper young men and women

71

did not simply go out on a "date," but rather, were introduced at an *o-miai*, a formal meeting with the clear intention of determining a person's suitability for marriage. Naokichi must have liked Kiyoe from the first moment he saw her, for he began to visit her regularly, though always formally in accordance with custom. One day the young engineer could contain his feelings no longer, and summoning up all his courage, he declared his undying passion for Kiyoe the only way he knew how. He began, "Two people working together toward the same goal are, I believe, like the wheels of a cart..." By this time she must have known him pretty well, for she did not ridicule his awkwardness, but simply lowered her head and replied, "If you are satisfied with me, that is all that matters." The two soon announced their betrothal.

On hearing of Naokichi's plans to marry, the Sakai clan was at first typically indifferent. Then, suddenly, they did an about-face. Kan'ichi even paid a visit to Naokichi's intended father-in-law and told him that he wanted to be on good terms with the Kobayashis even if the marriage did not go through successfully. His motives were all too clear.

The Kobayashis replied through their go-between that they were not opposed to the marriage, but that it was not fitting for Kiyoe to marry a man from a bus company. What plans were there for the young Mr. Sakai's future security and what plans had the family made for a residence for him and his new bride? Their only conditions were that Naokichi return to his family firm and that he and Kiyoe have a house of their own to live in. Kan'ichi replied that they would soon be transforming the factory into a joint-stock corporation and that the brothers would all share in the stock. As for a residence for the young couple, well, that was already in the works.

After his marriage in November of 1927, Naokichi quit the bus company, as he had promised, and returned to the Sakai Ironworks. The family built a small house on one corner of their lot in Kanasugi for the young couple to use. It wasn't impressive, but it would do.

Even after Naokichi was married and set up in his own house, things were still difficult. He was working hard day and night at the factory, and Kiyoe was little more than an indentured servant to her brothers- and sisters-in-law. She had to cook, draw water, fetch firewood, and wash clothes for the whole family. If they were all unmarried, she thought, it would be understandable, but all the Sakais (including Watanabe's children, who also lived there) were married, and all their wives treated Kiyoe like a housemaid.

She was a bright, strong-hearted girl, but eventually she felt she could take no more. She went home one day to see her father, who had always shown a soft spot for this daughter ever since she was ladelling out miso in his store. But if she went looking for sympathy, she was un-prepared for his response. "How is Naokichi doing?" her father asked. "Fine," she replied, "although he works like a slave at that factory." "Well, then," old man Kobayashi replied, "As long as Nao is giving it everything he has, you have no choice but to do the same, no matter how painful it may be." She was surprised, but her father's tone was gentle and kind. "And you can always come home and live with us," he added with a smile, "Whenever Nao says you're of no use to him." She went back home, determined to stick it out however long it took.

On Sept. 18, 1928, Naokichi and Kiyoe had a son whom they named Kuniyasu. He should have been their greatest joy, but it seems he was trouble right from the first. Kiyoe's delivery was very difficult, perhaps a portent of what was to come. A few months after he was born, they discovered that the baby could not turn his head to one side. An orthopedist told them it was a stiffened muscle in the neck and it must be massaged daily. Kiyoe took the boy to a masseur every day, rain or shine. But that was just the beginning.

Long after he should have been running around the house, the boy still hadn't learned to walk. A diagnosis at Tokyo University hospital showed that both thigh joints were dislocated. He was taken to another famous orthopedist for physical therapy. This, too, had to be continued without any break, and so poor Kiyoe had to carry

The author as a child.

him to the doctor every day for six long years. Of course, the boy was still growing all this time, but could not walk properly by himself. Although he was much too heavy for Kiyoe to carry easily, she would not complain. Every day she faithfully carried him to the doctor, ignoring the weather. At age six an operation was necessary. And then another. There was some doubt the boy would ever heal completely. Kan'ichi endeared himself to Naokichi and Kiyoe even more by offering his own advice: "The kid was born crippled, he'll stay crippled. Why spend all that time and money on him? Find him a job he can do sitting down."

By the time Kuniyasu finished elementary school he had undergone six operations on his hips and three on his neck. He had still another operation later on. Eventually his legs began to strengthen and he could walk fairly well although not perfectly. His parents encouraged him to participate in running events at school. "Of course you will finish last," Naokichi said, "But that's not the point. You must enter the competition and fight with all your might. You are not competing against others." They took him skiing and he cried all the way down the mountain, but eventually he learned, and gradually came to enjoy it. Both his parents understood something of the value of suffering to achieve a better life.

On His Own

In 1933, after much deliberation, Naokichi and Kiyoe felt they could no longer remain a part of the family company. Despite all Naokichi's hard work, he was getting nowhere and was still treated badly by one and all. When he announced his intention to separate from the Sakai Ironworks, Kan'ichi and then even Watanabe flew into a rage. "If you leave, you give up everything," his brother threatened, "You won't get a penny!" Naokichi wondered what had happened to Kan'ichi's promise to Kiyoe's father to turn the firm into a joint stock company and to make Naokichi a director. But he did not complain. He had made up his mind to leave, and if that meant forsaking everything, so be it.

Naokichi set up a factory in the Shinagawa section of the city and called it Sakai Ironworks. His brothers complained that he was no longer connected in any way with the family business and so could not advertise as a branch of the family firm. He renamed it the "Sakai Precision Machine Shop" and opened for business.

There couldn't have been a worse time to go independent. 1933 was the low-point of the Depression years. Like many other enterprises, he found no customers and no business. Times were terrible, but Naokichi and Kiyoe were happier than ever before. They were free, they were together, and they were proud parents. Naokichi used the time to design new machines for the day when business would pick up. All the same, they were penniless. Just keeping the shop going and finding enough for themselves to eat was an effort. One day brother Taro dropped by. "Still no customers?," he laughed. "Tough break, you know. We've got so much business we're turning people away. Don't know what to do with all the customers." He smiled and went away. Naokichi tasted the bitterness of his decision to break away from the family. Still, being free from their nasty jibes and shabby behavior was worth any price. Or so he thought.

All this time the Sakai Ironworks had continued to produce new gears and sold its products for tremendous profits. Had its president been a man of vision, had he constantly encouraged his men to come up with new ideas, the firm would be famous even today. However, Kan'ichi was not such a man. Since the firm was doing so well, he decided at the age of 40 to follow his stepfather into retirement. This he did in a most characteristic way: He simply cleaned out the safe one day, saying "I get all the money. The rest of you just keep on working." No one could complain, as this was his legal right as sole heir. He then built a comfortable home in another section of Tokyo and enjoyed his wealth. He had ten children, but none of his sons went into the business, and none of his daughters married with the idea of bringing a husband into the business. It was as if he had found a good trick to make money and it had paid off. Once he was rich it was time to get out and enjoy his fortune—the company was of no lasting importance.

For Naokichi, though, his business was everything. Win or lose, he and Kiyoe would bet their futures on the little shop. Finally, he was able to secure a contract. It was for highly precise optical machinery and fulfilling it would put food on the table for some time to come. Try as he might, however, the crude machines he had at his little shop were not up to the specifications the customer required. So he went back to Kanasugi, back to the family shop to ask for permission to use the sophisticated equipment there. The reply was unambiguous: "You are no longer a part of this company or this household. You will never use this equipment so long as you live."

In June of 1934, with their son just entering elementary school, Naokichi and Kiyoe celebrated the birth of a daughter, Michiko. The sufferings of the past year seemed to fade into the distance. The birth of another child, rather than adding to their burden, seemed to give them strength. Surely things would get better from now on.

In the following year Fusa died. This was in some ways the cruelest blow to the young couple, for she had been an endless source of support to both of them. Kiyoe suddenly remembered how after Kuniyasu's birth she had found some money tucked away under her bed, a secret present from

Fusa. In her last days Fusa must have been happy to see that Naokichi was at last on his own and now with a loving wife and two children around him. Still, after all the torments at the hands of his brothers and their continuing callousness towards him, she must have worried for her youngest son. On her deathbed she whispered to Kiyoe, "Take good care of Nao," and pressed money into her hand. Kiyoe refused, but Fusa insisted she keep it. Kan'ichi eventually found out about it and tried to make Kiyoe feel guilty. He even ordered her to turn the money over to him, but Kiyoe refused. She would burn it before she would hand over to him any fraction of what Fusa gave her. How much longer, she wondered, could this misery continue?

Then one night Naokichi was startled by a vivid but odd dream. It left such a strong impression that upon awakening he had to tell his wife about it immediately. "I was swimming in a river, and I saw a large, beautiful carp. For some reason I wanted it more than anything in the world, but I was sure there was no way I could catch it. Then, somehow I got a hold of it. I was so happy, it's hard to explain. Then suddenly I woke up." Kiyoe smiled. She said there was no question the dream was an omen, a portent of the future, and a very good one at that. Their luck was about to change and Naokichi would catch the carp for which he had waited so long.

Shortly thereafter, Naokichi had a chance to

meet with his best friend from his Municipal School of Industrial Arts days, a fellow named Tadashi Ayabe. Ayabe had gone on to the Science Department of Tokyo University and was then sent to America to study the latest in precision machinery. He was now the head of a new Precision Machinery Department at the nation's most advanced technical research center, the Physical and Chemical Research Institute. In the course of their conversation, Naokichi told him about breaking away from his brothers' business and of his current struggles. Ayabe, rather than commiserating with his old friend, looked pleased. For he remembered well Naokichi's outstanding mechanical skills and his passion for detail. He realized at once that this was the man—and the shop—to produce the kind of high quality precision machinery that the Institute would soon need. He suggested the idea to Naokichi, but his friend was typically honest, explaining that his shop was still small and poorly equipped, hardly the kind of place to be producing equipment for the prestigious Institute. But Ayabe reassured him that what the Institute sought was superior skill and experience, not a big factory. Whatever production machinery was necessary could easily be purchased once the Institute began placing orders.

Ayabe did begin placing orders for experimental machinery and instruments, and the orders kept coming. With this steady business guaranteed, not only was Naokichi's shop rescued almost overnight, but he had a customer who appreciated quality and demanded the most of his abilities. Later, the Institute decided to market its own line of machining equipment. Once again, the orders went to Naokichi. All across Japan manufacturers jumped at the chance to obtain high quality machinery endorsed by this prestigious institution, and soon Sakai Precision had more work than it could handle. Naokichi, who couldn't drag a customer in off the street a few years before, had to rent a nearby building just to store his inventory.

Four years after breaking away from his brothers' shop, Naokichi decided it was time to build a big plant of his own and equip it with the most modern machinery available. With the help of his friends at the Institute, he was able to secure a bank loan, and with the money he built his new factory. Here, in the late 1930s, he immersed himself in his work.

His son, Kuniyasu, would wander into the factory to watch his father at work. What toy or game could possibly compare with the sight of his own father pulling a piece of red-hot metal from the fire, placing it on an anvil, and showing a group of apprentices how to strike it to achieve the proper shape? "A man needs a spirit of iron to work with iron," he would say while beating the hot metal. His workers would look on, often uncomprehending, and then try to emulate their master. Clearly, Kuniyasu's father possessed unusual skills for a man of his time, and so it was

A typical milling machine produced by Naokichi's shop and sold by the Physical and Chemical Research Institute.

fascinating to watch him work. Yet it was also painful to see this genius with metal and machines who had so much difficulty in communicating his knowledge to others.

In many ways he was a hard man to work for. A perfectionist, he did everything himself, and he expected everyone around him to work as hard and as skillfully as he did. Even when he tried to teach others how to do something, it was usually in curt, sharp tones, expecting his subordinates to catch on immediately just as he would have in their place. He always thought that other people should naturally be able to do anything he did, when in fact none of his workers could keep up with him. It is easy to see why he sometimes drove other people crazy. At times he was actively disliked, but his staff respected him tremendously, even when they couldn't always get along with him. Those who left to join other firms inevitably rose through the ranks quickly wherever they went, mostly as a result of what they had learned at the Sakai shop, and many a manager came back later to thank him.

Kuniyasu, too, felt this same respect and awe for the man, and was embarrassed to fail in his father's eyes. One day the young boy discovered an electric socket hanging from an extension cord. He stuck in his fingers and got the shock of his life. Despite the pain, he could not tell his father—not because the old man would be angry, but because he felt ashamed that a factory-owner's son should have done such a foolish thing. Someday, he knew, when he was much older, his father would expect him to learn the business and to take over management of the Sakai Precision Machine Shop.

One day Watanabe, Naokichi's stepfather came to visit. He asked to be shown around the plant, and was very impressed. Afterwards he joined Naokichi alone in the drawing room. There he bowed deeply and apologized for the past: "I never expected you to amount to anything. You have done well. I am truly sorry for the way I treated you." Naokichi said later he began to forgive the old man then and there, but neither he nor Kiyoe could ever forgive Kan'ichi.

And so the years went by. Some of the top corporations in Japan became Naokichi's customers, and finally the Physical and Chemical Research Institute paid him the greatest compliment of all—they offered to buy his company. And they were very persuasive. They would pay a very large sum of cash, Naokichi would still be president and all the workers would be retained. He thought about it for some time, but in the end he refused. Of course he knew he could have become extremely wealthy in a single day, but he decided it would be better to be the master of his own fate rather than anyone else's employee, however well paid.

There was another reason, however. It had to do with his philosophy of business. Naokichi had seen other small firms taken over by big ones

Naokichi Sakai, a master of machinery, was equally accomplished as a husband and father.

and seen many destroyed by their sudden growth. He felt that when big companies take over a good little business, it begins to grow for no reason, extra employees are hired and the company begins to lose its drive. Keeping things small, using the minimum number of personnel, and always pushing to reach a target guaranteed a sharp, professional organization, one where every man felt part of the company's total effort. That feeling was impossible in a bigger organization, which meant the workers would stand to lose rather than gain if the firm were sold. Naokichi couldn't phrase all of these ideas clearly at the time, but he knew in his bones that it was wrong to opt for the ease of big company life.

The Institute's machinery division was privatized and continued to work closely with Sakai Precision. Orders kept flowing in, but by this time not all of them were for private industry. Some of the equipment was purchased by the Navy, and Sakai machinery found its way onto battleships instead of factory floors. Although these were good days for the company, they were not good years for Japan. And Naokichi, absorbed in his work as usual, could not see the dark clouds forming on the horizon. The war, just a minor skirmish in China when Naokichi was getting started, had grown into a worldwide conflagration in just a few years. The war would change Naokichi's dream forever and launch another generation of Sakai into his own business.

Part II
KUNIYASU
REMEMBERS

Putting Our Lives Back Together

As the tide of war began to turn, life for ordinary citizens like my parents became more precarious. In Tokyo, people had never known such terror. The waves of B-29s came over the city again and again, and the horror of their incendiary raids is impossible for me to describe. It was worse than the worst nightmare. Every time a squadron of planes came overhead, you had to run into the fields. Trains were useless, merely targets for the airborne gunners. The wooden capital was methodically destroyed, not by explosions but by fire. So many people burned to death or were suffocated by the flames that you could not count the bodies. The survivors were more dead than alive, more like lifeless mannequins than men and women who used to live down the street. Overnight the city became a charred, rubble-strewn wasteland populated by zombies and thieves.

From the very first attacks, my father worried constantly about evacuating the family. First he sent my little sister, Michiko, to a seaside town some distance from Tokyo. Then he packed up all the family's possessions and loaded them into three boxcars bound for Niigata, even farther from the capital. Things would be safe there, he thought. But the train was an easy target for the bombers and two of the three cars containing all our belongings were burned.

We had built a bomb shelter behind the

house, but it did us no good. One beautiful April day the bombers came while we were away from home. Our house and factory were both hit and everything, including everything in the shelter, was incinerated. Had we been hiding there at the time, we all would have been burned to death. It is a sheer miracle that we survived while tens of thousands of others perished.

I was 16 when our house and my father's shop and equipment were destroyed. All that Naokichi had worked so hard to build up was consumed in but a few moments. I can still remember another sight: the hens that we used to keep in front of the factory all charred black and lying on their sides, like burnt decoys scattered by the bomb blasts. He picked them up one by one, cut away the charcoal that was once flesh and exposed some edible meat. This he spread around so that what few pets were still alive in the neighborhood might have something to eat. As I watched him silently cutting open our dead chickens, I felt for the first time that my father was somehow like a warrior of old. Surrounded by the ruins of a life's work, shapeless lumps of melted machinery and smouldering embers of his factory, he was mentally preparing to do whatever was necessary to preserve his family or die in the process.

He took us away from that inferno, up to the mountains near Nikko, northeast of the city. My high school friends in Tokyo were all impressed into labor service, but I escaped this fate by going with my parents to Nikko. We rented rooms from a friend and lived Spartan but relatively quiet lives. Planes would often fly overhead, but there were no targets to bomb in the country, no incendiary attacks on the rural cities, and no nightmares that fed on our sleep. Most fortunate of all, we had enough food to stay alive while multitudes were hungry in Tokyo. It was a frightening, miserable time for us, but nothing compared to the massive suffering that engulfed the capital. We even began to think that the realities of war might pass us by. Then one day we were told to dig air raid shelters, and we knew that the terror had found us even out there in the mountains.

Before the digging had begun, however, we were notified that there would be an important broadcast at noon. I still remember everyone gathering around the old radio, fearing even worse news to come. Then from inside that wooden box came the sorrowful voice of the Emperor. His first national address was made to announce the end of the war and Japan's unconditional surrender. I am embarrassed to admit that my very first reaction was typical of a spoiled high school boy: I was overjoyed that I wouldn't have to dig an air raid shelter!

But the end of the war did not mean the end of misery. The clock did not suddenly go backwards, dead friends did not come back to life, the injured were not suddenly healed, and the lives that had been destroyed could not simply be re-assembled. The end of the war meant only that we would no longer have to run away from our ruined homes and hide ourselves in holes. Our friends in Nikko made it clear that we were welcome to stay there for several more months, perhaps that it might even be a wise idea. But our family had lived in Tokyo for centuries, through fires and earthquakes and other disasters. We wanted to return, even if only to wreckage, as soon as possible.

My parents arranged for me to stay with a friend's family so that I could go to school. When I showed up for my first day of classes, there were no textbooks. Many of the students were wearing military uniforms, having no other clothes left. Yet I still did not comprehend the privations that the survivors were facing. That evening I went home to our friends' house and found a warm bowl of rice (a great rarity in Tokyo those days) and a bowl full of cooked vegetables on the table. In the countryside such things were not so uncommon, so I took no special notice of the hot food. Tired from my first day at school, it was no trouble at all for me to polish off both bowls in short order. It was only the next morning that I discovered I had eaten the entire family's meal. I was so embarrassed I knew I had to leave.

I moved in with my uncle Taro (Naokichi's brother), but he, too, was barely able to stay alive. Watching him crush beans one at a time with a pair of pliers or pound unhulled rice in a bottle with a bamboo stick, I realized how frighteningly poor Tokyo had become and how many people were living on a knife-edge between life and death. All the insurance everyone had paid for all their lives was suddenly worthless. Investments were meaningless, government bonds were no more than fancy paper, and neither pre-war wealth nor social position guaranteed food on the table. I think we were most shocked to learn that even relatives of the Imperial family were impoverished overnight. What chance did ordinary people such as ourselves have?

I left Uncle Taro's home, but it was very difficult to find any place to live. So many buildings had been destroyed. At last my parents found me a small upstairs room belonging to one of the local shrine offices in the Gotanda area. My father had to go to the black market to buy decent food, but he said nothing. My mother cooked it and made sure I ate regularly so that I would be strong enough to go to school.

The end of the war also brought massive inflation. More than anything else, we needed a real house. Naokichi owned a piece of land in Ohta Ward, and he still had a little cash, but prices for everything were rising so fast that money seemed almost meaningless. Finally, he was able to hire a carpenter, and within a year we had a small place to live. But life in Tokyo was still unimaginably poor. I still remember how on one side of the house we put up a bamboo fence tied together with copper wire. Early on the first morning we saw that the fence had collapsed: someone had stolen the wire during the night. We replaced the copper with old rope and the fence stayed up. I also remember we decided to build a simple stone wall in front of the house. First, we had to make dozens of trips to the ruins of our old house to pick up stones for the new place. Then we had to take turns sitting up at night in a small hut just to keep an eye on the stones. In those days even a pile of rocks was fair game for desperate thieves.

Luckily, one of my friends from elementary school happened to live nearby. Hiroshi Sekiyama, hearing that we were moving in, volunteered to sit up in the hut with me and guard the stones. In this way my family came to know Hiroshi, and we all began to depend on him for many things. I believe that Fate ties men together in strange ways, and no surer proof is needed than my friendship with Hiroshi. I had no idea what invisible thread connected the two of us, but even then I knew that we would remain close for years to come. How close I could not have imagined.

My father salvaged an old pump and some pipe from the city's rubble, we dug a well and the house had water. It was a step back towards life as we used to know it. I suppose the worst casualty of the war was neither our house nor factory but our spirits. All of us were mentally numb and hard put to be enthusiastic about anything. All of us, that is, except my mother. With her usual energy she inspired the family to muster its reserves and start acting like a family again. "We're going to rebuild the business, aren't we? Kuniyasu, you must continue studying and help your father. Michiko, you must go to school and learn everything you can about the world around us." So life began again. Michiko went off to a girls' school, I went back to Waseda High School and my father began taking stock of the ruins of our his company.

My mother found simple piece-work for a nearby electric-accessory maker. It was very easy work and terribly poor pay, but it meant we could all sit around the table at night and talk while we worked. It did not escape my notice that where once my father had been the principal subcontractor for a nationally famous firm, now our family was at the very bottom of the post-war subcontracting pyramid, putting little pieces of electronic parts together in our home at night. I guess I was also beginning to take an interest in the way businesses operate. During my summer vacation I got a job with a small neighborhood electric insulator dealer and tried to learn all I could from his shop. I watched him carefully, studied his negotiations with customers and suppliers, and began to see how small businesses function. Some day, I thought, when my father has rebuilt the Sakai shop to its former glory, I must be ready to accept whatever responsibilities are given to me. I must study how a modern business functions, how to buy and sell, how to deal with employees and so on. Even as a teenager, I was beginning to prepare mentally for a moment far in the future when I would inherit the family business.

A 'Sun' Is Born

What I hadn't counted on was how much damage the war had done to the parental 'generator' that powered our family machinery. In 1947 my father called me to him and turned my world upside down. I can't remember what I was thinking about as I went to see him, but my thoughts evaporated when I saw the serious look on his face.

"Kuniyasu, I have something important to say. Listen to me carefully," he began in a very formal tone. I could not imagine what earth-shaking words he could have for a boy of 19 who had just survived a war. "I have worked hard all my life, and I have been fortunate," he continued. "When I started my own company I had nothing. Over the years I built it into a very solid business, which I hoped someday you would take over. Even a few years ago I felt I could begin to think about retiring. I had saved some money, more than enough for your mother and I to live on, and I was planning to step down at the age of fifty. I thought I could relax at last and enjoy life, secure in the knowledge that my family was well provided for and that my company was growing steadily." He paused and looked away for a long moment. When he began again his voice had changed. "Now I find that at the age of fifty the war has taken everything I have. Everything I've built, everything I've saved, everything I've worked for is gone. Perhaps I should grit my teeth once again and start all over from scratch. I don't know ... I am not an old man, but I feel old. I have worked hard and I am tired. When I look around, many of my friends and the world I knew are gone. This is not the world in which I grew up, it is a very different place. Perhaps it is a place better suited to young, energetic men full of dreams." He paused again and reached behind him.

"Here is our bank book. There is some money in the account, but with the way inflation is soaring and the currency likely to change, it may be worthless in just a short while. Do not count on it for much."

I was dumbfounded. What was he getting at?

"I urge you to start up the Sakai machinery business again. But if there is anything else that you think you can make a business of, I will support you completely. I have no intention of retiring and becoming a burden to you. I will work as hard as I can and I will help you in any way that I can. But from now on you are the head of the Sakai family, and its future is in your hands. I know I can trust you."

As I have said, I was nineteen years old, a

student who had been spared the real horrors of war in a mountain retreat, not even drafted into forced labor like my peers. I often had food when others had none, and a roof over my head when many were homeless. Suddenly I realized how I had been insulated, not only from the worst of the war years, but also the worst of its aftermath. Now, with the war over, I felt safe because I expected that my father would take care of the family no matter what. His sudden announcement came like an earthquake, pulling away the stable ground I had taken for granted. Of course, I was young and eager to prove myself in the world, but I had always counted on his leadership and his inspiration to be my guide. Now he wanted me to lead. He expected me to be responsible, not just for my own future, but for that of my parents and my sister. For some silly reason I found myself remembering the time I stuck my finger in the electric socket.

Since my total real-world business experience was what I had gleaned from a summer job, I decided to get some education as quickly as possible. Over the radio I heard about a course being offered at the Tokyo Metropolitan School of Industrial Arts, the same one my father had attended long ago. Unfortunately, there wasn't a machinery course available, only a painting course. In 1947, though, you couldn't be choosy. It was rare to find any kind of decent instruction in any usable skill. So I signed up for the painting course.

There were about a dozen people there, some in military uniforms, some dressed as shop workers, but I was the only high school student. After a few weeks I decided this was going to have to serve as the basis for starting a new business.

Looking back on it all now, I guess my father was right in thinking the times were suited to young men short on experience and long on dreams. When I finished my classroom work, I announced that I was going to start up a painting business. My parents, whatever they may have thought, were totally supportive, and introduced me to people who had such businesses. Fourteen years after my father had declared his independence from his brother Kan'ichi and opened his own shop, the Sakai family started their second business on the same site. Amid the ruins of Sakai Precision Machinery we built a new 'plant,' a flimsy wooden structure, but to me a real factory and the beginning of the biggest and best painting company in Japan.

Although it was normal to name a firm after the owner or the family of owners, I rejected this idea. I believed that a firm is not the possession of one individual, even if he starts it or inspires it. A company reflects the people who keep it going. I decided to name my new firm for the sun because I was filled with optimism and wanted to build a bright new world for our family from the debris of the old. On August 15, 1947, I inaugurated the Taiyo ["Sun"] Painting Co.

I gathered together all the materials I could find to start up a painting business: one furnace, a couple of spray guns and hoses and one ventilation fan—not much with which to build a new world, but I was elated. It didn't take much talking to persuade my old friend, Hiroshi Sekiyama, to quit his job. He moved right in to the plant, taking up a room on the second floor with a cheery, "I'll be your caretaker." So there were two of us, plus two workers who had agreed to leave Mitsubishi Heavy Industry and join the venture, plus my father and mother for support.

Our business was simple: We spray-painted things. Anything. Match box cases, opera glasses, portable safes, you name it. If someone had contracted us to paint a Jeep or a baseball stadium, we would have done it. We were learning as we went along. Little by little we got the hang of it, but we weren't very confident of our work. When we finished a batch of work, Hiroshi and I used to load the finished goods on a cart and pull them over to our customer. Then we'd turn around and hurry back just in case they decided to return the order while we were still in sight. Fortunately, no one complained about poor workmanship, but it was very difficult to collect money for our work. Here my mother, the family business manager, was invaluable in negotiating with our customers and getting us what was due.

Mother also introduced us to an old family friend, the former manager of a good painting shop and an expert in lacquering work. Under his instruction, we learned all about coating techniques, and we began to take on higher quality projects. Soon Taiyo Painting was coating everything from phonograph pickups to auto dashboards and window frames. We couldn't believe it—we were actually in business and doing well. That is, doing well for a couple of kids with almost no equipment, experience or connections. But what we lacked in the basics we more than made up for in enthusiasm. And luck.

For example, a very sensible law requires that every painting shop have a fire extinguisher. However, finding a working fire extinguisher in a city that had been fire-bombed was a futile task; we might as well have been panning for gold. We couldn't find a workable unit for any price, and this minor detail threatened to shut down our new enterprise. Then one day my father and I were walking through Ginza. We decided to take a shortcut down an alley littered with rubble. As we walked on, talking about the problems that needed to be overcome just to keep Taiyo in business, Dad stumbled over something. On closer examination it proved to be a real, fully charged fire extinguisher half-buried under a pile of debris. We looked around. It clearly did not belong to any of the businesses on either side, so after a moment's hesitation we picked it up and lugged it home. I wondered not for the last time if someone was looking out for the Sakai family.

I could not keep working and also go to school, so I decided to quit school. This should have been a truly momentous decision for me. After all, my father had endured much just to be able to go to school, and I was in one of the most prestigious schools in the country. If I had continued on from Waseda High School to Waseda University, my classmates would have surely become heads of industry and important government officials. But I was not thinking about such worldly things. Truth to tell, I was already in love with the idea of working for myself. Despite all the sleepless nights and the hard work, I loved my little company and I wanted to see it succeed. I honestly felt that to be out in this "new" post-war world was as important as anything else I could be doing. Just before I quit school I made a grandiose speech to my classmates about the need to experience the "real" world and how I would be there to hire them when they got out. They must have thought I was crazy, and perhaps I was. My foolish words sprang from the idealism of youth, but my deep feelings of pride and satisfaction at seeing a little company grow remained unchanged despite the many years that followed.

Hiroshi

Hiroshi and I were both caught up in the intoxication of running a company, but there were

The birth of the Bunsha Group: the author with his best friend and partner, Hiroshi Sekiyama, both 19 years old.

times we both wished our business was something cleaner. The two of us were constantly covered with paint, not only our clothes but our hair as well. We could easily pass for a couple of bums with our newspaper hats and paint-covered faces. In fact, I think our appearance would have surprised wartime refugees. If we were asked to dress like that today, it would be next to impossible to find rags that dirty. We often had to take the train to our jobs (no small company at the time could afford a car), and it was truly embarrassing to be seen looking like a couple of paint-stained beggars. But we had no choice. Once I remember the train lurched so violently that our paint cans spilled all across the floor in a crowded car. I could have died of shame a dozen times, but we just had to grin and keep going.

We advertised that we would accept any kind of painting work, which meant we were offered a lot of unusual jobs, but we needed the work so we were happy to take them. We painted giant iron tanks bigger than a swimming pool, and gas tanks and restaurants. Once, we were asked to paint a metal tower about 70 feet high and 15 feet across. Today such a job would simply mean erecting a scaffold around the tower and spray painting it. But we had no scaffold, only short wooden ladders, so we tied the ladders together with rope. Not surprisingly, they collapsed again and again and both of us nearly broke our necks several times. Around this time I began to notice that whenever we had to paint a dangerous section, Hiroshi would send me away, saying "I'll do this part. You go back down and figure out what we should do next." I was beginning to realize what a remarkable friend I had found in this quiet, stout-hearted guy.

Hiroshi's father had been an innkeeper, but he died while Hiroshi was still quite young. His mother remarried and his stepfather was very hard on him. Hiroshi had almost no one to call family other than his sister Yoshiko, whom he worried about constantly. Once he even asked me to marry her, telling me again and again what a good girl she was. Yoshiko came to live with him on the second floor of the Taiyo building. Only about a week later she fell very ill with an infectious disease and everyone was terrified. Everyone except Hiroshi, that is. He stayed by her side day and night, but to no avail. She died a few days later, leaving him more alone than ever.

One day my father called both of us to him. We were still young and insecure, and I suppose we both worried that we had done something wrong. He spoke in a formal tone, just as he had a couple of years before in this same room. "I have been watching you two. Your work is progressing, your company is struggling, but it will survive and grow in time. I have no doubt about this. What I have been noticing more recently, though, is the way the two of you work together. You have very different characters, yet you work well as a team.

106

Kuniyasu, I suggest you recognize the extent to which Hiroshi is helping to make your business prosper." I felt embarrassed even as he said the words, for indeed I could not have kept the business alive without my friend's constant and eager assistance. "I further suggest that from now on you share the responsibility for the company equally. Whether it succeeds or not is both of your responsibility. Be partners in name as well as in spirit."

How could my father have seen into both our hearts—and our futures—so clearly? I will never know. But from that day forward Hiroshi and I became partners, and we have remained partners ever since.

Kids, Cars, Bankers, and Work

If it seems that my life was entirely caught up in my little factory, I cannot deny it. There was not much time for anything else. I did find time, however, to attend an *o-miai*, the ceremony in which a young man and woman are formally introduced with the intention of arranging a suitable marriage. In fact, I went to four *o-miai*, as I remember. The first three girls turned me down flat. When I look back now on my youth, my prospects, and my total devotion to my work, I almost wonder why they bothered to meet me in the first place. But then on the fourth *o-miai* I met a very special girl named Mitsue who was the same age as I. For whatever foolish reason, she decided to throw in her lot with mine, and the two of us were married in the autumn of 1950. My parents were delighted, hoping that marriage would make me more settled and responsible. They needn't have worried, for I was already married to my little company and that was making me more responsible by the day.

The first hint that our firm was starting to do well came in a roundabout way. Other painting shops began to spread rumors that Taiyo was no good, that we were just a couple of kids trying to swindle unsuspecting customers. We were furious, but we knew it was a good sign. Now we had to make sure our work was top quality and our reputation would surely spread. We slowly began to invest our meager profits back into the business. First we bought a telephone, something none of our rivals had. This enabled us to have much better and more professional-looking contact with our clients, who were now larger and larger companies. Then we gradually gave up painting water tanks and such, and concentrated on more specialized work inside our factory, including baking and coating processes. But we still needed something special, something to announce that we had arrived. We were hungry for business and we wanted to let the world know that Taiyo Painting would go the extra mile for its customers —literally. So we bought a car.

Of course, it wasn't much of a car by today's standards, just a little 3-wheeled job with no top, more of a glorified go-kart than an automobile. Still, when no shop such as ours had a vehicle, it was a very impressive status symbol. Until then we had always piled our finished products onto a wooden cart and hauled them many miles to make deliveries. Sometimes the cart would get stuck on a muddy embankment as we were about to cross a river and the whole load would go tumbling down the hillside. I'm sure our repeated heartbreaks on occasions such as those helped us to rationalize splurging on a car, and even today I have fond memories of those old Mitsubishi 3-wheelers.

Since it was an open car, you got soaked when it rained or snowed. It had no battery, so you had to pump-start the accelerator, and it had no steering wheel—you had to steer with a metal bar. All the same, it turned corners like a rabbit and was a lot of fun to drive. We took jobs over a hundred miles from Tokyo thanks to this rickety little car. We also tempted Fate several times because of it. Once I almost skidded off a frozen mountain pass at night, and many times I was almost frozen myself driving the damn thing in the winter. Despite all the problems, though, the little car was a boon for business. We soon found we were getting all sorts of new orders simply because of our mobility. We eventually bought two more.

What I remember less fondly than the

sprightly 3-wheelers is the high-handedness of the Japanese banks. As inflation continued to rise, the Bank of Japan tightened its monetary policy, which put a severe squeeze on the economy. Collecting money from our customers was tough, but getting loans from bankers was impossible. I still remember as a young man with a growing business the frustration of being turned down by loan officers time and time again. They would lean back in their chairs and say smugly, "We don't have any money for you. We have better customers." I always left the bank burning with rage. After all, if somebody was going to turn me down for a loan, at least he could be polite about it. But in a nation trying to get back on its feet, bank officials felt they were somehow appointed to run the show. It was like some kind of disease they all shared (and one which did not improve for decades, believe me). Eventually I got my loans thanks to various government-related agencies, and our company was ready to expand.

Taiyo Painting Co. then began experimenting with different kinds of coatings, different kinds of techniques and equipment. Of course, we were still in the process of learning our business, but we were also acquiring some good customers along the way. Some of Japan's leading camera and electronics makers were now sending in regular orders. Taiyo was beginning to look like a real company, although you couldn't tell by looking at its executives. We were working all day and part of each night, and we looked it. Despite our increased cash flow, all our money went for payments of one sort or another. At the end of each month there was nothing left over. Which was OK with the two of us: we had neither time nor money for recreation, so day after day all we did was work.

In 1951 my first son was born. For the first time, my chronic cash shortage began to hurt. My wife had to stay in the hospital an extra week until I could scrounge up enough cash to pay the bill. We named the boy Yuta, which means something close to "child of the Sun." Mitsue and I thought that was appropriate, both for his life in this new world and as heir to the Taiyo vision.

In the same year I also decided to change the name of my company. Through my business contacts I saw many firms in Tokyo that needed all sorts of work, not just painting, and I felt that Taiyo should branch out to profit from this increasing demand. I hoped that an early diversification would help the little company to grow more quickly. And so "Taiyo Industry Co., Ltd." was born. I thought the name was sufficiently broad to cover whatever work we might do in the future and it was still faithful to my original "Sun" concept. Thus, at the heady age of 23 .I was experimenting with corporate diversification and image changes. I would like to say that this was because I was a far-sighted chief executive who was years ahead of his time, but the truth is I simply wanted to expand our range of business and (hopefully) attract more customers.

And attract customers we did. We put up a 10' X 16' billboard next to a major railroad line to advertise our new company name and the fact that we now had two lines of work, painting and stamping. We built a pressing plant adjacent to the painting plant, and orders came in right away. Like our painting and coating orders, however, they demanded high quality and careful attention to technique. Unlike the painting business, however, neither Hiroshi nor I had any idea how to achieve such precision with the unfamiliar machines. As usual, this didn't stop us from trying, sometimes with laughable results. When we first started doing press work, for example, we needed a set of die blocks. Hiroshi spent a lot of time and effort trying to develop a set, with upper and lower blocks measured precisely so that they fit perfectly. But when we started to use them the dies bit into the metal sheets and stuck. It was some time before we discovered what everyone in the business knew: it is necessary to leave a tiny gap between the upper and lower dies so that the metal sheet can fit between them. We were beginning to realize that our endless reserve of youthful energy simply couldn't make up for our lack of experience in the field of machinery.

But there was someone else in the family to whom a shop full of humming machines was just like home. Until then, my father had tried to stay out of our business. Painting was not something he knew much about and he probably thought it better to let us build our company and learn from our mistakes. But when we decided to set up a factory to handle mechanical work, he could no longer resist. He began helping out as our handy-man. He was always around the machine shop, making sure all the equipment was in perfect order, devising new tools for our workers and finding ways to make our jobs easier. I think he was very happy to have a shop to work in and to see both his son and Hiroshi, who was almost an adopted son, making a success of their business. Looking back on it now, we were amazingly lucky, for without his help our new business would have failed in the first six months.

Even with my father around to rescue us time and time again, I often wondered why in the world I had rushed into this metal working busi-ness. Yet whenever I found myself wishing I could simply give up and go back to what I knew well, all Naokichi had to say was "When I was your age I wished more than anything in the world that my own father was still alive to help me," and I would forget my complaints. Indeed, I was fortunate in many ways.

All this time our main business was growing rapidly. There were many other firms in the field, so there was a lot of competition. Some of the bigger companies were tough to compete with because they had the capital to invest in new equipment, such as large baking ovens. We also needed this equipment, but as I've said, the banks were less than cooperative. In the same year that we changed the company name we built a second addition to our main factory. I decided it was time for us to have the same kind of equipment as our rivals, so we scraped together the money to buy a big, modern oven. I can still remember how proud Hiroshi and I were the day they came to install that oven. Our first major capital investment, the beginning of a new age for Taiyo.

When we fired it up for the first time, some gas leaked and the thing exploded. It blew open the door and knocked one of the technicians across the room. He wasn't seriously injured, which is more than I can say for my pride.

Despite such mishaps, Taiyo kept on growing. We soon had about 50 full-time workers in three buildings and were starting to send simple preparation work outside to people in the neighborhood. I remembered just a few years ago when my mother used to take in piece-work and we'd all sit around the table helping her to do it. It wasn't a full-time job, but it was a good way for her to make some money on the side. So I promoted the idea of sending work out to local housewives, giving them some part-time income and easing the load on our regular staff. In this way, Taiyo had already established a simple subcontracting chain. We received half-finished goods from outside our shop, finished them in-house, and sent them on, either to our clients or to other firms in the chain.

Although this system was not so common in the painting business, it became the foundation for almost every kind of manufacturing business in post-war Japan. Everything from automobile parts to transistor radios was started at the lowest level, passed upwards to a small processing company, then upwards again to an assembler, and on and on until the so-called "maker" put his name on the product and shipped it. In time, Taiyo Industry would grow to become a leading player in the electronics version of this subcontracting system, but in the early fifties we were still learning how it was done.

First Signs of Success

Business began to pick up around this time. Not only our business, but the economy as a whole. The Korean War had started and the Japanese economy was beginning to show some signs of life. In 1952, the government formed a national telecommunications monopoly and launched a series of 5-year programs to develop that industry. I was particularly aware of those developments because a fair amount of our work was coming from electronics makers wanting their products coated or plated. As the electronics industry grew, Taiyo grew. Our little 3-wheelers were making deliveries several times a day now. We were getting more orders and bigger orders. Soon all our oven capacity couldn't handle the amount of work coming in. We needed a new, really modern oven, and a large one at that. But we couldn't afford it and no one would lend us the money. After some thought, I ordered the factory expanded once again. We would build our own oven.

The ever more remarkable Hiroshi offered to design it and some of our workers pitched in to build it, and soon enough we had a brand new industrial oven. Much to our surprise (but not Hiroshi's) we found that our home-built oven was every bit as good as the big expensive ones our rivals were using. Ours was just as safe, too, and a lot cheaper. Both our quality and capacity increased measurably. As if to confirm our success, even our machinery orders started increasing. The new painting plant and oven were hardly finished when I had to start construction on a new machine shop. I even splurged and ordered our first steel-framed structure. We were starting to look like a pretty successful company.

With all these orders pouring in, you might think we had developed some exceptional techniques that created great demand for our work. Far from it. While the quality of our work was good and still improving, our most outstanding feature was our willingness to learn. We bid for jobs that we had no idea how to complete. We knew we had to learn as we went along, and we were willing to learn the hard way. Sometimes we would bid on a project for a big client. He would ask to see samples of our work in that particular area, and we would dutifully take them over for his engineering department to examine. The engineers would break out laughing at the sight of what we had done. Did we give up and go home? Not on your life. We'd ask the client's engineers to show us what was wrong with our work and explain in detail what was needed to make it right. We read books on machine work, on precision soldering, deep drawing techniques, annealing and so on. We invited the authors to come talk to us about these techniques. Looking back now, I am absolutely amazed at our willingness to launch into new fields and fly by the seat of our pants.

In the mid-fifties television sets gradually began to appear around the country, although they were still quite rare. Wherever a TV set was installed for the public to watch, such as in a train station or the window of an electric appliance shop, a big crowd was sure to gather. And when something like a baseball pennant series or a sumo tournament was on, the trains could come and go unnoticed while hundreds of passengers stood transfixed in front of the glowing screen. As you can imagine, our factory had no time for recreation of any sort, and our workers, many of whom lived in the plant, spent most of their waking hours on the job. So I bought a TV and put it in the dining room of our house for everyone to enjoy. After work all the live-in staff would gather in front of the set, eating dinner as they watched their favorite sports shows.

To us there was nothing special about the president of a company eating or relaxing with his employees, and anyone who suggested such a thing would have been laughed at. We were all in the same boat together, and Hiroshi and I were hands-on working managers more than executives. We liked it that way and so did our staff.

As our financial situation improved, we were able to make some bold investments in new equipment. We got some large orders as a result, and the firm just kept on growing. Part of it, as I have said, was just luck, but part of it, I cannot deny, was due to our strategy. For example, many large clients ranked the work they needed done into three categories, A, B, and C, and allowed their subcontractors to choose the type of work they wanted to do. Some of our flashy rivals opted for "A" work, the most precise, the most exacting, and the best way to display their superb techniques. Taiyo elected to do B and C-type work. What happened? Demand for the most specialized work was slim, while the vast majority of products required ordinary levels of skill but large volumes. Consequently, Taiyo was flooded with orders, and our plants were busy night and day.

Although I was not conscious of it at the time, in the back of my mind there was always the fear of fire. Our main plant was a large wooden structure full of flammable paints, thinner and solvents. On one side of the building we were spraying flammable liquids while on the other side by the ovens gas jets were burning all day. It was a recipe for disaster, and it began to obsess me. Whenever I heard a siren at night I jumped out of bed and called the fire station to find out if it was our plant. If I got off the train at our station and saw the red lights of fire trucks on the move I would run like a crazy man all the way to the factory, fearing the worst.

We did have several fires, though mostly small ones. One of the most frightening was a fire that started in the loft of the machine shop and threatened to spread to all the other buildings. Everyone was paralyzed with fear until Hiroshi shouted to the workers, "Bring me a ladder quick!" then scampered up with our big old fire extinguisher in his hand. He calmly looked at the fire, read the instructions on the old cannister as if he were reading a textbook, then set about methodically extinguishing the fire. What else would you expect?

Indeed, Hiroshi proved himself to be something special time and time again. I think I mentioned earlier that my legs were weak and the thigh joints deformed from birth. To help strengthen them, my parents had started me skiing when I was in first grade. They thought the sport would be good for my legs and allow me to enjoy a sense of mobility that I had never known. I grew to enjoy skiing, and one day I took Hiroshi out on an overnight ski trip. He was a total novice, but as usual, ready to learn. He shot down the slopes like a maniac, and before long he broke his leg. The next day there he was at the factory, cast and all, making his regular deliveries in a 3-wheeler. On other occasions he had a high fever and was so sick he couldn't stand up, but he would always appear at the factory no matter what. For such a gentle, soft-spoken boy, he had the spirit of a warrior. I was glad that my father had urged me to make him a full partner, and even happier that I'd had the good sense to ask him to join my foolish endeavor in the first place.

In the spring of 1954, four years after my own marriage, Hiroshi married and we became brothers. That is to say, he married my sister, Michiko. She was happy, he was happy, I was happy and my father was delighted. Hiroshi was always enthusiastic and optimistic, but not in a foolish way like his own son. Hiroshi was quiet, yet open and sincere, always ready to help others, but never looking for credit for himself. It is no accident that I am writing this history of our company rather than he, for he would no doubt say that it was all my doing or perhaps merely the hand of Fate that built Taiyo, and would forget to mention that he had any part in it.

By the mid-fifties the firm was growing steadily. When I was 28 we gave up our reliance on the little 3-wheeled cars and bought a new Toyota light van. This may sound unimpressive today when every little corner store can afford a delivery truck, but at that time it was a very big move for a company of our size. The next year we bought a passenger car.

That was also the year we coated a pair of special decorative microphones to be used in the Diet, Japan's national legislature. We had been coating cameras for some time, but this was a special job demanding both quality workmanship and artistic design. Hiroshi created the finish, a beautiful brushed satin pattern modelled after the design of 15th century Chinese bronzeware. Our staff felt a deep sense of pride every time we saw the Diet in session on TV, for there were our microphones clearly visible on the main podium.

Death (and Birth) of a Salesman

As Taiyo Industry Co. entered the sixties, it had grown into a medium-sized company of some renown. I felt it was time for the firm to start looking more like a corporation and less like a family shop. Among other changes, Taiyo's work was now divided into technical and sales divisions. Since attracting new business seemed to be the top priority for the coming years, I took charge of this new Sales Division.

I think it is common knowledge that the field of sales is fiercely competitive. Companies spare no effort to snatch an order from their rivals, and a salesman is evaluated only in terms of the orders he brings in. One weapon in the battle for customer loyalty is clear: technical support for whatever equipment is purchased. Another is an ill-defined range of activities called "customer service." In Japan, customer service is assumed to include a very large amount of wining and dining and every other form of entertainment imaginable. The purchasing agents for big companies expect to be treated like visiting dignitaries, their every desire to be provided for by the eager-to-please salesmen of potential clients. This may not be the most cost-effective system for establishing business relations, but it is a firmly entrenched practice among all levels of Japanese business.

Now, I'm the kind of person who likes to speak his mind, so I'm not very good at flattering people. Moreover, I was never a drinker, so the prospect of spending endless nights in bars did not seem very attractive. However, because I believed that sales promotion was essential for our company's growth, I assumed that such a life would become part of my job for a few years. What I didn't know, having never done this kind of work before, was how totally it can take over your life.

I took customers to bars, clubs, any place they wanted to go. Since I wasn't much of a party-goer (spending all your time inside a painting factory is not the best way to hone your social skills), and since I didn't know one bar from another, I let my customers choose their favorite places and dutifully followed along, picking up the tabs along the way. In time, I came to know the night life of Ginza as well as most. I was acquainted with dozens of expensive bars, fancy nightclubs, cabarets and geisha houses. All of this was quite an eye-opener, even for a man of thirty running his own company.

The funny thing was that my parents still treated me as if I were in high school. My father would often be waiting by the gate when I came home late from the Ginza, often with stern words about keeping more regular hours. Eventually he gave up, not because he grew used to my carousing, but because he realized that sales work in a real company meant more than just visiting clients during business hours. But things got worse. Soon I was spending every night out—and enjoying it. I am embarrassed to admit the sales work had become just an excuse for indulging in an exciting new life with many pleasures.

One morning I returned from a weekend outing, tired but happy. My mother handed me the following letter without a word:

Kuniyasu,

You have forgotten that we are fighting a war, a business war. Each day the battle starts at 8:00 am, but Taiyo starts without its general, for he is still comfortably in bed, exhausted after a long night of carousing. He thinks that money can buy anything, including his soldiers' loyalty. Since he is paying their wages, he assumes the men will love him and do their jobs without complaint. But do these men work for money alone? How happy they would be if their boss were around occasionally with an appreciative word or two. Just a sign that he was proud of them and respected them would lift their spirits, increase efficiency and help us produce better products.

But no, you can't be bothered with the responsibilities of running your own company. And that is typical of you. Ever since you were young you have always tried to escape from things you didn't like, to run away from problems. So far you have been lucky. Someone else has always been there to cover for you. Thank God for your father, for Hiroshi, for your wife Mitsue. How much longer are you going to count on them to do your work, to handle your responsibilities?

When I look at the company now I get the feeling that no one is in charge. Of course I know that sales promotion activities are important to our success, but what is the use of all that effort if the company falls apart while you are away?

Love your company more. Love your factory. If you really love it, you cannot be away from it for more than an hour at a time. This is your only castle in the world. However small it may be, it is yours and you are the lord here. You may say it's all right for you to be away because you trust others to work in your place. But is that how they see it? No, they feel that rather than trusting them, you are taking them for granted. People who feel unwanted start to look for other places to work. This lord may one day lose his castle, all for a few glasses of *sake.*

You know I love you, and I still believe in you. You know what must be done, whether you like it or not. Think not only of yourself, but also of your son. What kind of company do you want to leave him? What kind of role model do you want to set for him? Your presence in the factory is essential. As long as you are president, you should be absent only in the direst emergencies.

Think carefully about what I have said,

Your very concerned mother

It seems that while I was out having a good time, Hiroshi was sweating away in the factory, often till late at night. As I have said, he was a very hard worker and didn't mind putting in extra hours night after night, but he was running out of patience with a "partner" whose idea of working all night was spending hard-earned company funds in plush watering holes with ladies of the evening. Now that Taiyo Industry was healthy and prosperous, he reasoned, perhaps it no longer required his services. Now that he was married, he had responsibilities to his family as well. Wouldn't it make better sense to leave the 'family' business, just as Naokichi had done years before, and start his own firm? With this in mind he went to my father for advice.

Naokichi listened to Hiroshi's plans in silence. He understood perfectly where the problem lay and what to do about it. He said to Hiroshi, "If you truly wish to leave, I will give you half of our assets right now. You deserve them. But if you leave, this company will be the worse for it. I wish you would stay at least a little longer and allow me to have a word with Kuniyasu."

Kiyoe then took my sister Michiko aside and reassured her that family loyalty should not complicate her responsibilities towards her husband: "You must follow Hiroshi whatever his decision. You must be prepared to share his lot no matter what may come your way. If times get difficult, he will need to know that you are always there to help him in any way you can. That is how it should be with husband and wife."

My father then summoned me. As always, he was direct and to the point, his tone flat and rational as if reporting some event in another city. "Hiroshi wants to leave and start his own business ... As you know, Hiroshi has no parents, we are his family. He works harder than anyone here, he always does a good job, and he is always cheerful. You, on the other hand, spend most of your time in downtown bars, having a good time while Hiroshi is working in the factory. Who do you think is more valuable to this company? I am sure any father would feel as I do, that Hiroshi behaves like a true son and that you have gone astray. Should I ask Hiroshi to stay here in your place? I do not want to do that, but you are making the decision very difficult for me. In the end, the responsibility for this situation is in your hands, as is the solution. Think about it and we will talk again."

I was crushed. I was hurt. I knew my father was right, but I couldn't admit my own laziness and irresponsibility, even to myself. How could my own father talk of throwing me out of the house just for trying to do a good job as a sales manager?

The next morning, rather than deal with the situation sensibly, I went straight up to Hiroshi and told him that as of that moment I was taking over the factory work and he was in charge of sales. Then, without leaving any instructions as to how he should handle the purchasing, deliveries or any of the other things that went with the job, I stormed out of the factory. Hiroshi had no idea what my father had said to me and even less of an idea how to deal with all our clients. But in his typical unflappable way, he simply went to Nao-kichi and asked if he could start the sales side from scratch and do it his way.

What had sprung from my childish temper tantrum turned out to be a big plus for the company. For with Hiroshi's natural friendliness and humility, he soon proved to be a born salesman. Customers loved him. He was always thinking of what they needed and how to help them rather than pushing what we had to offer. Just being around Hiroshi made people feel good, and that, of course, is the best sales tool of all. The end result of this foolishness was that I went back to the factory where I belonged, Hiroshi went out and found all sorts of new business for us, and Taiyo continued to grow.

The Taiyo Game System

By the end of the 1950s, though, we discovered a problem that almost all small-company executives must sooner or later come to terms with. We had lots of business, orders were coming in steadily, and the company was growing, but we had no cash. Our customers were beginning to tighten their subcontractor systems, which meant we were now paid less per unit for our contract work than in previous years, while our labor costs and other overhead were increasing steadily. The result was painfully obvious. Our profit margins were getting squeezed between these two opposite pressures.

I lost a lot of sleep trying to figure out how we would get out of this profit "crunch." Labor costs seemed likely to continue rising, and there was little chance that we could persuade our clients to pay more for the same work. If anything, they were likely to increase their pressure for us to lower costs in the months ahead. Within a year or so Taiyo's accountants would be doing some painting of their own—in wide lines of bright red ink. I continued to rack my brain for an answer.

The "answer," of course, was perfectly obvious. I had to find some way to increase productivity. What was not so obvious was how to achieve this. The usual approach is "top-down" pressure: Management demands increased quotas while at the same time trying to hold wages at current levels. This is fine in theory—the company gets more work per employee, which bring unit costs down and increases profits. What the theory doesn't provide for is the reaction of the employees. How would any of us feel to have an employer say "More work from all of you! 50% more this month and another 50% next month!" Even if he offers to increase salaries slightly, the simple command that everyone will now work harder is onerous. And if salaries are not going to change, the employee feels not like a valued member of a corporate team, but simply another body pulling an oar on the corporate slave ship. The foreman shouts "More! Faster!" and increases the beat of his drum. Taiyo had never been that kind of a shop and I was determined it never would be. So I continued to rack my brain for a way to increase productivity without decreasing employee morale.

And then one day I remembered how my father always said, "If a man is responsible for his own work, he will do a better job." This led me to think that if all our staff had the feeling that they were not mere employees, but actually responsible in some way for the well-being of the company itself, they would both work better and enjoy it more. This is human nature. A motivated worker is a better worker. But too many managers try to motivate by employing some kind of threat. Fear is a poor motivator for a group of people trying to work together to achieve a common goal. However, when a worker has real incentive, when he is committed to doing his job better, when he is given a freer hand in how his work gets done, the end result will always be improved performance.

One of my early business mentors had told me "Divide profits beforehand, not afterwards," but I had forgotten. Now it all began to make sense. The answer for our company, I decided, was not tougher management, but less management. Workers instinctively ask for more money and try to get by with less work because they see themselves as mere drones on a payroll. By turning that situation upside-down, by giving them not only a share of the profits, but effective control of their own work schedules, you let workers determine their own salaries. This was not a radical revelation in terms of world economic history, perhaps, but close to heresy in Japanese business at the time. Who cares, I thought, as long as it gets results? Besides, I liked the idea of letting workers decide for themselves how their work should be done. I would tell them exactly what our profit situation is, give them a share of those profits, and let them decide the fate of Taiyo Industry.

So I devised the "Taiyo Game System." I called it that because I wanted the workers to compete with each other to improve their productivity, but not in a life-and-death business struggle. I wanted the competition to be fun, like a game. We divided the staff into small autonomous groups. Each group was in charge of an entire "cycle" of work, from obtaining orders to delivering products and collecting payment. The groups were like small companies, each one competing with the others to achieve higher results for the same kind of work. We posted the results for each group's efforts on the factory walls. And, needless to say, groups of employees were rewarded monetarily for their success in surpassing normal monthly quotas.

Was it successful? No, it was extremely successful. Our staff was suddenly re-energized. They worked harder, performed their jobs more meticulously, and were far more concerned than before with how much their individual efforts were either costing or benefitting the company. Everyone was on the go. Everybody wanted to check the graphs on the wall and see how they were improving. Those in charge of sales practically ran from one client to the next, while those in production would check and double-check their orders for any signs of defects, then offer their finished work to the customer's inspectors for approval. It was as if some unstoppable work virus had infected the whole company. Most of all, everyone seemed to be enjoying it. People worked harder each month, but cheerfully so, then lined up to see the results posted on the wall. We assigned various workers to be Game Director and Game Supervisor and rotated the positions. From the employees' point of view, work had become both challenging and fun. From a manager's point of view, it seemed like a dream come true.

But most impressive, perhaps, was the view from outside. As far as our customers were concerned, the factory had somehow been reborn. We suddenly went from being a good firm with quality products to a super firm, devouring orders and returning defect-free goods on time every time. The word spread quickly among our old customers and our sales people found it easier than ever to collect orders. Newspaper articles about Taiyo's "game system" spread the story farther still. The company was suddenly inundated with new orders. Our factory was running at beyond what we believed was maximum capacity and still our order books were chock full.

From the workers' standpoint, the system was also a success. When we started up the "Game" we handed out one week's wages in advance. You might say we were priming the pump for worker expectations. Also, our staff felt that no matter what happened with this new game, they owed us at least one week's extra hours. As it turned out, they gave many months' worth of extra hours. Everyone worked longer, harder and more productively. They also looked happier than before and took home the fruits of their labors in their pay envelopes. For years after we implemented the game system, our staff were regularly receiving double their regular monthly wages in performance bonuses.

The end result was a more efficient workplace with a much higher quality (not just quantity) of production. When people are more flexible in their income, they can be more flexible in their thinking. Not only was the company better off financially, but we were a stronger, happier shop as a result. Business writers and university professors from all over Japan came to study our factory and its new compensation system. The nation's two biggest newspapers wrote articles about it, and even MITI (the Ministry of International Trade and Industry) came around to find out what we were doing. In its own way, Taiyo made history in the annals of Japanese corporate management.

Employees

In the years that followed, my father and I often talked about how a business should be run. We agreed that the ideal situation for a family company such as ours was for succeeding generations of the family to produce the most talented leaders of the firm. Yet we both realized that this was a foolish and conceited idea. Even our ancestors would not have wanted to maintain family control if their descendants were not men of talent. So we felt we must hire young people, train them in the ways of our company, and let them experience the ups and downs of business cycles, and the inevitable problems of working in a small company. Then let them mature into good managers. In business, Naokichi used to say, man is the most important asset.

We began after the war by recruiting young men fresh out of junior high school, then later out of high school, and taught them the business from scratch. I believed then that people need responsibility to learn, and that they learn better by doing than by studying. I no longer believe that—I know it. We found out again and again over the years how true it is simply by putting bright young people on the job and letting them "discover" their work. The result? They learned their jobs quickly and took an interest in what they did. I knew from long ago that this is one way to avoid "big company disease." Many big firms have elaborate systems for training new employees, but people in those firms report that as the personnel systems become more complex and more orderly, the workers tend to become less interested in their work and more "mechanical" themselves. Naokichi and I agreed this was one of the worst fates that could befall a company, and we both sought ways to avoid it.

Unfortunately, I had never run a company with a large staff before, so Taiyo had to learn about hiring personnel the hard way. In the early days, when we were desperate for workers, all sorts of people came to us. Most were good men, but every now and then we would hire some quiet-looking, respectable sort only to find out later that he was an itinerant trouble-maker. I remember one soft-spoken fellow quite well. When his time came to leave us he walked into my office without saying a word, drew a large, ugly-looking knife and placed it on the table between us.

"I am from this kind of world," he said carefully, "And when I leave an organization, I am used to getting a little something as thanks for my services." Obviously his salary these many months did not qualify as "a little something." I thought for a moment. We didn't want a reputation for giving in to extortion, and yet... I decided that avoiding trouble now was the better part of valor. I passed off a bottle of rare, foreign whiskey I had received as a present and a few small bills, and he left with a nod. Fortunately, such troubles went out the door with him.

For every troublemaker, though, we were blessed with a platoon of talented people. One fellow I knew who worked for another firm dropped in for a visit one day. I noticed he looked depressed. He said that he was unhappy with his firm's management and had decided to quit and seek employment with a different firm. But before leaving his company he had gone around the workshop testing every piece of equipment, replacing all the loose bolts and nuts, tightening screws, oiling all the machinery. He made sure that the equipment would be accident-free for years after his departure. I thought that this man was the kind we could use and I made him an offer. He eventually became president of one of our Group companies.

It is sad but true that most managers never really know how all their employees feel about them. Thus, I was surprised and pleased to receive a vote of confidence from my staff in a most peculiar way. The Labor Standards Bureau apparently heard that Taiyo Industry workers, including its female staff, were putting in tremendous overtime hours. Since at the time women were often exploited and forced to work long hours for low pay, the officials were suspicious of a serious infringement of the law. They came to the plant and investigated thoroughly, interviewing every member of the staff at length. Needless to say, no criminal charges were filed. But after the in-

vestigation was over, the official in charge told me
that something remarkable had caught his attention. He had questioned nearly 100 employees in
private. He guaranteed them confidentiality, and
asked them to speak freely about the company and
its executives. What complaints did they have,
especially about the management? "Not one person had a bad word to say about either you or your
partner," he said. "How do you do it?"

I had to laugh. How did we do it? We never
thought about things like that. We treated all our
people as if they were friends or family, not like
hired help. This is one of the biggest advantages of
small companies, and the main reason my father
did not sell his business before the war. But I
needed to have the lesson brought home to me in
a dramatic way, and the government inspector's
comments opened my eyes. I began to see the
importance of keeping a company at a "managea-
ble" size.

Another kind of trouble led to the same
realization that we must be doing something right.
It came a few years later when two of our newer
employees decided to start a labor union. They
talked a few other workers into joining, then immediately petitioned a national organization, the
General Council of Labor Unions, for membership. In spite of their feverish campaigning at the
factory, though, no new members signed up and it
began to look as if their union was missing
something fundamental—worker dissatisfaction. I

met with the union representatives several times for some frank talks. It soon became clear that my own goals for our employees' welfare went far beyond the guarantees the fledgling labor union was demanding. I asked them to help me realize my dream of an ideal workplace for all employees. They were embarrassed. The General Council of Labor Unions decided that the fledgling union had misjudged the situation and ordered them to disband.

But the story does not end there. Some time later the same two fellows left Taiyo and went to an electronics company nearby where they started another union. The management responded to this perceived threat by taking the case to court, and in the resulting conflict the firm was closed for ten years. Two senior managers of that firm eventually came to ask me how we had settled our dispute with these characters so amicably.

I told them that my own style of management was more progressive than anything any union was likely to demand. If they believed me, they probably thought I was crazy. But my feelings about what is now referred to as "employee relations" have not changed since I was 19 and covered head to toe in paint. We have a saying in Japanese about the special relationship that grows among people who "eat from the same pot." It means that if you share certain basic experiences with people you can truly understand their feelings and their needs. Only then will they trust you. Our employees had seen Hiroshi and myself sweating side-by-side with them so many times in the factory, had enjoyed happy times with our families, and endured tough times with us when the company went through all sorts of problems—to try to stir up trouble in such a shop is like trying to start a labor union in an ant colony.

I suppose we were lucky to have hired so many good people in the first place, and luckier still that we all got along so well year after year. Again, I was struck by the importance of working in a place that operates on a relatively small scale, not some gigantic factory where no one knows anyone else. You can't build real worker loyalty in a factory that looks like an army camp, I thought. Little by little the message was beginning to sink in.

Diversification

In 1959 we built a 3-story factory on our old plant site. The building itself wasn't so remarkable, but what was inside marked a turning point for our company. On the first floor we continued to pursue our main lines: painting, coating etc. On the second floor we added administrative offices. But the third floor was devoted to a new project, experimental work relating to condensers.

It may seem odd for a painting company to start fooling around with electronics, but in our

Mr. Hiroshi Sekiyama. Friend, partner, brother-in-law... none of these describes the importance of Hiroshi's contribution to my life or to the success of our companies.

case the transition came naturally. We had been coating all sorts of small parts for the hundreds of new electronic devices now being manufactured in Japan. As I looked around, I saw more and more companies committing sizeable resources to this new field, and I could feel the momentum beginning to grow. Electronics would become an increasingly important industry in Japan and those firms who went into the business early would prosper in years to come. And yet, I was still unsure of how best to proceed. Should we continue to focus only on coating these parts for other manufacturers, a business in which we had become quite expert, or should we enter this field on our own and start learning from the bottom up?

Around this time I was also beginning to formulate my own views of how to run a business. As 1960 approached, Taiyo was still doing well, but our order flow was unpredictable. Like most companies, our business moved in cycles. I wondered how a good manager should prepare his company to deal with such swings in business activity, and my conclusion ultimately led us charging into the electronics business.

I decided that to do well is not the most important thing in business—that is a given. The most important thing is to be prepared to do well no matter what happens to economic conditions around you. A really well-managed company will not merely endure but will even prosper despite constant changes in the surrounding economic environment. Today I believe that more than ever. The very rapid pace of technological change and constantly shifting markets have made it necessary for a company's management always to look ahead and be ready for change. Whole industries can become obsolete overnight. Planning for change means survival. You have to watch not only your own business but your competitors' as well. If too many companies expand their facilities at the same time, then cut-throat competition is just around the corner. Then you've got to keep an eye on the government's monetary policy. Once a recession starts, it tends to snowball quickly, and the government will tighten monetary policy even if it strangles a lot of smaller companies. A manager who wants to stay in business can never be caught off guard.

In any case, I came to the decision that Taiyo was strong, but still needed to be much stronger. Adding another side to our business, especially in a fast-growing sector such as this new electronics field—would help to shore up the company against future economic downturns. And so I gave the OK to begin simple work on condensers in 1959.

The 1960s will always be remembered, not only in Japan, but around the world, for the mass commercialization of electronics. It was a time when bulky vacuum tubes vanished and tiny transistors took over. Everything electronic shrank, both in size and in price, and this started a proliferation of consumer electronics unimaginable just a decade before. Compact color TVs pushed large black-and-white cabinets out of the living room, kids carried transistor radios to the beach, and, for better or worse, the electric guitar changed our peaceful world forever. Japanese electronics makers discovered huge, insatiable markets overseas and began flooding international markets with exports. The domestic market also boomed and the electronics business became a new pillar of modern Japanese industry. And as that business grew, Taiyo Industry shifted more and more into the manufacture of electronics parts.

It wasn't a sudden change. It started small, like the electronics boom itself, then picked up speed. For example, one of the key components in many electronic products was the printed circuit (PC) board. One day one of our clients asked us to help him with the production of printed circuit boards. He said we should be able to help since we were familiar with coating work. He also made it clear that this order would not be repeated, and that they would do the work themselves when their new factory was completed. But as electronics-related production soared, our client found his firm inundated with orders for PC boards and had to keep us under contract for some time. Of course, I didn't want to do just part of the work, I wanted to try my hand at producing a PC board in-house. I was sure that with a little study and a little hard work we could make the things ourselves.

Our client was totally opposed to this idea at first, but as his business grew he could no longer keep up with demand. Finally, he gave in and let us handle the whole process of making PC boards.

Since we were not a big electronics shop, we had nothing but old, second-hand equipment to work with, totally unfit for handling this kind of work. Did it make sense to recondition them for what might never turn into much of a business? I had a hunch it would. So our staff reconditioned the machinery and brought them up to state-of-the-art specifications. Soon we were making our own printed circuit boards, and as the years passed that became our new main line of business. We learned more and more about the process and in the next decade captured over ten percent of all the PC board business in Japan. Not bad for a little painting firm.

Of course, we also learned a great deal about producing other kinds of devices, which set the stage for today's Bunsha Group and the enormous variety of high-tech equipment that we manufacture. But in the early days the problem was making the jump from producing a small part to producing the whole unit. Like the client who didn't want us to make whole PC boards at first, the big electronics makers didn't want us to handle more than a fraction of their production process. They said they wanted each subcontractor to be responsible for a single step. One excuse for this was to insure quality control, but the real reason was to guarantee that the subcontractors would never learn how to make the final products and thus become rivals of their parents.

By this time I had made up my mind about the problems inherent in big corporations, and I had no desire to become another Matsushita or NEC. Still, I was fascinated by this electronics business and frustrated that we were confined to its periphery. I felt that if we were going to get into the game at all, we should go all the way, as we had with the painting business. If that meant starting small and learning as we went along, fine. That was the point of the whole thing. If we had to hire specialists to teach us how to do certain things, fine. But we must learn the business top to bottom and inside out. Otherwise, we would forever be at the mercy of some other company saying "Don't do this, don't do that, you might learn too much."

I wanted more. I dreamed of doing everything: processing the sheet metal for some electronic product, coating it, manufacturing the condensers and PC boards, assembling the components, wiring the final unit and testing it. I even offered this complete "turnkey" subcontracting package to our clients. What could be better—we build it, you sell it. They said no way. You do this part, and company A does this part, and company B does this part, and we'll put it all together and market the product.

I started thinking, "If I don't get a little

creative here I'm never going to get to do the whole thing." I began to think about a new strategy. Instead of having all the divisions of my new electronics firm under one roof, I planned to set up a separate company for each division. This way each new company could grow and expand on its own. The idea of integrating several different companies appealed to me, as did the idea of keeping each of the individual firms small enough to benefit from what I had learned were the blessings of small-company management. Over the years I experimented with this idea of company division and gradually the modern Bunsha Group came into being. But now I am jumping ahead of my story.

It Helps to Know the Future

Every executive of a small firm worries about the future of his company. Will it survive? Will it prosper? For me there was never much doubt, even in the early days, mostly because I was young and optimistic. But as I grew older and business conditions became tougher, I was concerned about our future success. In particular, I was hoping that our new strategy of gradually shifting away from the painting/plating business and towards the electronics field would be a source of growth for the company. But with so much at stake, one cannot help but wonder.

And yet, I had few doubts that our company would ultimately succeed, even thrive. This was not only because I believed in our people and our products, but also because of two "prophecies," one in a dream that came to me and one from a man whom I sought out.

The former was very similar to my father's prophetic dream back in the 1930's, although I could not interpret it clearly at the time. Shortly after I established Taiyo Painting and I was chronically short of cash, I dreamt that I was swimming, and sure enough, I saw a beautifully colored carp. And then another, and another and then dozens of them. And I caught one after another and tossed them onto the shore. I filled my arms with them, catching as many as I wanted, until I was exhausted. When I awoke I knew it must mean something good for my little company, just as my father's dream marked the beginning of his firm's success. Yet I had no idea how accurate this prophecy would later prove.

The second prophecy came from a most interesting gentleman by the name of Hata. Mr. Hata was an ordinary-looking, unassuming man, unremarkable in most ways except one: he was a clairvoyant. He "saw" the future clearly and accurately time and time again, and despite his lack of interest in publicity, his reputation spread. For example, in the midst of the war Hata "saw" Japan's total defeat just a matter of years away. He was foolish enough to mention this to people around him, and sure enough, word reached the military police. He was arrested and taken before the local Captain (who had considerable power over what to do with citizens who maligned the government). Hata's reputation had preceded him, however. The captain summoned him to a separate room for a private interrogation. "You dare to say that His Imperial Majesty's forces will be defeated? When do you claim this will happen? Tell the truth or you will suffer the consequences." Hata was terrified. A truthful answer could land him in jail—or worse—but if the Captain had already heard his prediction from other sources, to lie now would cause him even more trouble. He decided to tell the truth: "In August or September of 1945."

There was a brief silence as the Captain considered the prediction. Then his voice softened. "Hata-san, tell no one else what you have said here today. And from now on please confine your predictions to the weather—for your own sake." Then the Captain gave him a bottle of whiskey as a present and ordered him released.

Hata not only survived the war years, he kept on making predictions, no matter how outrageous they seemed at the time. Years later he predicted the demise of a famous Japanese corporation. People thought he was crazy. The firm was as solid as a rock, a giant in its industry. Surely Hata had lost his touch. Then, in 1964 the company went bankrupt.

In 1963, shortly before that event, I sought out an introduction to Mr. Hata. I asked him about a number of things, but principally about the future of my company at this important juncture. He told me not to worry and predicted great success for Taiyo, but only on the condition that we make a very minor change in the way the firm's name was written in Japanese. I considered his advice, but was still a bit skeptical. The next year his prediction about the other firm's bankruptcy came true, and shortly thereafter I changed the way our company name was written. In the years since, I feel it is safe to say his prediction of our success has proved accurate.

Throughout the 1960s and '70s Taiyo grew tremendously, and as I had hoped, evolved from a general painting company into a high-tech electronics company. Along the way it spun off numerous other companies, forming a group of several dozen firms which is still growing. This process began more or less by accident, but proved to be such a valuable strategy for the optimum management of both people and business that I began to take it more seriously. I cultivated it, experimented with it, and after several years I had perfected a management system which I call *bunsha* (company division). This is the basis of my management philosophy, and I have written about it in some detail in another book (*Bunsha*). For those who wish to know more about that system and how it developed over the subsequent two decades of Taiyo's history, I recommend the story contained in that volume.

Here let us simply say that in 1978, at the age of 50, I resigned as president of Taiyo Industry to devote my energies to the future of the Bunsha Group of which it is a part. I told my successor to start splitting off the operating divisions of Taiyo Industry into separate companies so that they would be revitalized and could grow with the same energy as the firm did when Hiroshi and I were still paint-spattered executives. Then I rented an office in Ginza, where visitors can find me easily (and from which I can easily get to the Kabuki-za to see my favorite plays). Today Hiroshi and I are still there, sharing offices side-by-side, and meeting with people from all over the world who wish to learn about our system.

Naokichi's Legacy

Until the day my father retired, he thought only about work. He was a perfectionist, and totally absorbed in whatever he set his mind to. But after his retirement my mother took over. She had an interest in old Japanese folk songs and she set about teaching him. As you might imagine, my father was shy and not at all the singing type. "You want me to do what I'm no good at" he would say to her, but whatever he did, Naokichi always devoted himself to it completely, and so in a fairly short time he became an accomplished singer. The two of them travelled around Japan learning folk songs and meeting people, and once even appeared on TV to show off some of the songs they had "collected."

My mother also got him into social dancing. Was there anyone less likely to take up social dancing? If you knew him you would have laughed at the thought, and yet you would have believed it in an instant when you heard that he'd bought a pair of dancing shoes. If he was going to do something, he was going to do it right. When he got the travel bug, he couldn't stay put. My parents not only travelled all over Japan, they also went overseas (not a common thing at the time). They visited the U.S. and Europe, the Soviet Union, Hungary, New Guinea, and so on, and my father made friends everywhere. He wanted to visit South America and Africa, but he never got the chance.

In 1969 the old man found that his own machinery was defective. Unlike all the other mechanical devices in his life, this was one he couldn't fix. The diagnosis was cancer of the bladder. He had three operations in less than two years. Many of the workers donated blood for him. Still, he kept losing strength. I said to him jokingly, "Remember, our temple is Sengaku-ji. Don't forget it and get lost later on the other side." But he smiled only wanly. We both knew the end was near. One day he said to me, "I thought I would never forgive my brother Kan'ichi for all the terrible things he did, but now when I realize I will soon be going where he is, I think I can forgive him."

I suppose I never realized what an impression my father had made on people, but when a local physician closed his clinic for more than a week to stay by my father's bedside until it was over, I began to see how strongly people felt. He died in the summer of '71.

I cannot begin to express what an inspiration he was for me, even in his later years. One day many years ago he found me quite upset because some employees had quit. He said, "You just hire more men, you train them and you keep going. When you run out of patience to teach others, you are finished. You can always find more men."

Naokichi was a maker of things and proud of it. He despised idleness. He was always active, always looking ahead, always preparing for the future. He said, "Don't believe the old saying 'Everything comes to those who wait.' Everything comes to those who hate to wait." Always wanting to understand how other people built things or operated machinery, he was actually studying computer languages in his last months on earth.

And until his very last days, he used to go to the Kabuki, just as he had in his youth. Once, I remember he went to see *Bunraku*, the classical puppet theater of Osaka. Many of the great Kabuki plots are actually adapted from Bunraku

plays (called *joruri*). The traditional *joruri* tells of
the pathos of common men, torn between what
their hearts demand and what their social duties
require. Looking back on it now, I can understand
how poignant these dramas must have seemed to
Naokichi, what a responsive chord they must have
struck in his own soul. And not only for himself,
but in terms of those he loved. In some of the
dramas, for instance, it is a woman who is torn
between love and duty—a revelation in its day.
Naokichi must have thought much of his mother,
Fusa, and the sufferings she endured to provide for
her family.

It was in the twilight of his life that Naokichi
said to me, "I regret not having seen more *joruri*.
There is something inexplicable about the artistry
of this form. Be sure you go to see them whenever
you can." My father knew that I had not suffered
as he had, and that the Bunraku theater would be a
kind of lesson for me. In time I, too, came to
appreciate the Bunraku as well as the Kabuki, and
have passed this on to my own son.

The author, Kuniyasu Sakai.

Afterword

When I look back on my life and the growth of Taiyo Industry, I am surprised to see that I did not succeed by following in my father's footsteps. Our family heritage is a centuries-long tradition of working with metal and wood, of hammering and forging and machining to create tools and equipment. My father, like his father before him, was a machinist and an inventor. Had the war not intervened, I would surely have taken over his machine shop, although my own inventive talents would not have sustained its reputation for very long. Instead, I turned to the first opportunity that came along, started my business in another, unrelated field, and only later found my way back to his world of manufacturing.

And yet, in a real sense, my father helped to build Taiyo Industry from the very beginning, for his strength of character made me what I am today just as surely as he made anything else. He always believed in me and counted on me to succeed. When I was young, I was always weak and a bit frail. Dad used to take me hiking in the mountains near Tokyo every Sunday to help build up my strength. When I was very young he took me skiing and I cried all the way up the mountain, but with him there I learned to ski. He once said to me with a smile, "A good manager is born not made, but since I only have you to succeed me, we must hope for the best." It was only after I started to work with him that I came to see what kind of man my father really was. Always willing to do work others didn't like, or to do anything to make others' jobs easier.

In closing, I think it is appropriate to quote a line from a Kabuki play: "Whether you live for one hundred years or die unborn is merely your fate. There is no other path except the one set by fate."

I will keep walking on my path, knowing that my father is waiting for me further along.

K. Sakai

The Author and His Work

The story in this book provides a background to the foundation of the Bunsha Group, founded by Mr. Sakai and Mr. Sekiyama. Today the Group is one of Japan's leading diversified, middle-tier manufacturing groups, and comprises dozens of companies. While the core of the Bunsha Group is still concerned with producing electronic goods, other firms are involved in fields from gemology to aviation.

The Group's core companies produce state-of-the-art facsimiles, computers, laser printers, color copiers, and hundreds of other products for Japan's most famous companies. But much of the high-tech work is behind the scenes, in research and development and in component manufacture. New ventures include the importation and promotion of helicopters (the Group is one of the top importers in Japan), together with the training of pilots and mechanics to support the growth of this industry.

Although Mr. Sakai is still deeply involved with the affairs of the Bunsha Group firms, he is no longer directly responsible for their management. This gives him the opportunity to focus on new business development and on promoting his own management philosophy. He still enjoys meeting with executives from companies big and small to discuss management problems and how best to realize the ideals of corporate growth.

In the past several years he has travelled often to explain the system he calls *bunsha*. Recent speaking invitations have taken him back to Europe and the United States, where business seminars and universities often ask for his views not only on management, but also on the evolving structure of the Japanese manufacturing sector.

His article in the November/December 1990 issue of **Harvard Business Review**, entitled *The Feudal World of Japanese Manufacturing* generated considerable reaction in both Japan and America. Publications in several countries continue to request interviews with or contributions from Mr. Sakai, although his work and travel schedules make additional commitments increasingly difficult. He is currently preparing a new journal article which is scheduled to appear in English in 1992.

Anyone who would like to obtain a copy of *Bunsha* or correspond directly with the author, is welcome to write to Mr. Sakai at the following address:

Kuniyasu Sakai
No. 2 Kotobuki Bldg., 5A
Ginza 6-12-1
Chuo-ku, Tokyo 104
JAPAN